Cavalier

THE STORY OF
AN UNSOLVED MURDER
IN A SMALL TOWN

A True-Crime Memoir

CONNIE L. NELSON

George Gregory Nelson Publishing, LLC
Registered Agent: 201 3rd Street, Suite 1340,
Albuquerque, NM 87102-3368

First published in the United States 2022

Although this is a work of non-fiction, certain
official documents including the investigation notes,
probate documents and newspaper reports have
been utilized. In addition, personal correspondence
has been included.

The publishing company has no control over nor
responsibility regarding the websites and links in
this book. They were correct at the time of this
writing.

ISBN: 979-8-9856105-1-2 (paperback)
ISBN: 979-8-9856105-0-5 (electronic version)

Library of Congress Registration issued pursuant to
37 CFR §202.3

Case #: 1-11147317881

Sept 1, 2022

I dedicate this book to my husband, Roger, who
supported me during the three years of writing and
researching and also answered my questions.

Our dear friends Pat &
Bill Robbins live in Cavalier.
They have often mentioned
the murder, which happened
at a home not far from
theirs. Our last visit it
came up again and she
said a book had been
written about it. She sent
me this book and I will
make a note when done!

9-12-22 – Finished. talked to
friend Pat. She & Bill knew
all of the parties mentioned in

the book, or almost all. Bill
was an attorney in Cavalier
He lived there all his life.
Pat could not really
say "who done it". Many
of the possible "suspects"
are deceased.
Still unsolved to this
day.

Acknowledgments

I want to thank Lacey Hinkle for helping me with Cavalier town photos.

I also appreciate the support provided by Tim and Lynn Schroeder and the *Cavalier Chronicle* for permission to utilize their publications to tell my story.

I would like to thank Mary Neighbour and her company MediaNeighbours for being my book shepherd and editor.

Thank you to Pembina County Sheriff Terry Meidinger and Deputy Marcus Ramsay for sharing their insight into the world of law enforcement.

Finally, I'd like to acknowledge Attorney General Wayne Stenehjem for clarifying the North Dakota Freedom of Information process (FOIA), defining access to inactive investigations in 2004, and establishing the North Dakota Cold Case Unit in 2005. Unfortunately, Stenehjem died suddenly on January 28, 2022, at age 68. He had just announced his retirement plans.

Contents

Introduction

I REMEMBER THE LAST TIME I saw my friend Jack. We were in the hospital lobby, where we both worked. He was wearing faded-green scrubs and a lab jacket. He went through the door to the second floor. I never saw him again. That's how I remember him—going through that door.

This is a true story. My friend, Dr. Jack Wahl, was murdered in his home later that night. My life changed in so many ways that cold day in February 1986. This book explores my recollections, experiences, and memories while trying to make sense of this unsolved crime.

I've conducted research based on three main source materials: (1) interpersonal communications; (2) the investigation notes provided by the current Pembina County sheriff and his deputy; and (3) newspaper reports from that time, including the *Cavalier Chronicle*, the *Fargo Forum*, and the *Grand Forks Herald*. I kept these documents in an eleven- by thirteen-inch box, approximately four inches deep, which resurfaced when I retired in 2018 and was packing to move to New Mexico.

This is the box that contained the artifacts from the investigation, including newspaper reports and correspondence.

I knew right away what the box contained, even though I hadn't looked through its contents for many years. When I did go through the artifacts, it brought back a confusing combination of feelings and memories and a deep sadness. So many things had changed in my life between 1986 and 2018, with one constant: no one has ever been charged or convicted in my friend's murder.

Since I was retired and had time, I thought it would be therapeutic to write about my feelings as a friend of a murder victim, an unsolved case for thirty-five years. I have always been a writer: in marketing, advertising, and communications for thirty years, and as a grant writer for the last fifteen years. This is my first book, which I plan to publish in early 2022, the thirty-sixth anniversary of this open case.

Whether you live in a large city or a small community like Cavalier, the people who are left behind after a senseless death want to know what happened to their loved ones. This book has been written for those of us who grapple with murder, victimization, loss, and the unanswered questions—the friends and family of a victim of homicide who have given up hope of any resolution. I also write for two additional audiences: the fans of true-crime stories and the law enforcement officials open to suggestions about how to deal more effectively and respectfully with the victim's friends and families.

Sadly, Jack's case is one of more than two hundred fifty thousand unsolved homicide cases in the US today, so I am not alone. These murders remain unsolved for a variety of reasons. As time passes, the chances of finding the murderer are vastly reduced. But the idea that a case goes cold with no periodic review is hard to take when it's your friend or family member who's been murdered.

If you have had a loved one die suddenly, you probably know the heartache of not getting to say goodbye. When the sudden death isn't due to a long-term illness or a car accident, but instead an unsolved murder, it's like a wound that doesn't heal. And when the murder takes place in a small town, everyone you know could be the potential murderer—just one of the ways the crime changed my life.

Another way it changed was that I was forced to see myself from the police viewpoint: I was *just* a friend. If Jack had been a relative, I would have been included in the discussions with law enforcement, but I was not interviewed as part of the official investigation—and I felt I had a valuable perspective on Jack's life.

So, all these years later, I'm determined to conduct my own investigation and review of those tragic events. When I started writing this story, I realized that there were no follow-up stories in the regional media after December 1986, when Pembina County Sheriff Glenn Wells retired. It felt like the investigation was just sitting on a shelf, waiting for someone to discover it and reach some conclusions. Most of the individuals involved in the original investigation have since died, retired, or moved away from the Midwest, complicating access to the case records and the opportunity to interview key people.

The famous author and philosopher, Maya Angelou, once said, "There is no greater agony than bearing an untold story inside you."[1] After reading this quote, I decided that I should be the person to raise some questions about the investigation as Jack's self-appointed advocate, since after all, I was a writer and researcher and Jack's voice was silenced a long time ago.

That is exactly how it felt, like I had an untold story inside of me, and I needed to talk about it. So here it goes. I'm calling this story a true-crime memoir. I will write about how it feels to lose a friend to murder, and how the lack of resolution has impacted my personal outlook on life. This is *my* story. It is how I remember the events that led up to and followed Jack's murder. I have no intention of hurting anyone by including them in this story. I have simply selected key individuals because they knew Jack or interacted with him in some way. My main purpose is to try to make sense of this experience and to help others who have experienced the same anguish.

After all these years, I know now that I had a unique perspective as Jack's friend, and that has been my only motivation. I hope by writing my story, it can help others who find themselves in a similar situation, still grieving after all these years. Innumerable coincidences and life experiences have led me to this day.

1. Before Cavalier

My Story

I WAS THE OLDEST CHILD IN my family and the only girl—a built-in babysitter for my three younger brothers. We were all born in Breckenridge, Minnesota, hospitals because Wahpeton, North Dakota, and Breckenridge were "sister" cities, divided by the Red River of the North, and Wahpeton didn't have its own hospital.

The Red River of the North divides the Midwest states of North Dakota and Minnesota for two hundred miles along the eastern border of North Dakota. It is the only river that flows north in the US. Perhaps this explains the unique culture of the region? I have lived in five of the communities that adjoin this river border, so it might also explain my individual outlook on life. While the rest of the world flows south, I seem to be flowing north!

When someone asks, "Where are you from?" my response is usually, "the Red River Valley." Sometimes this flippant answer makes people uncomfortable. They really want to know where I went to high school or where my parents live. This book represents a composite of the places I've lived in North Dakota, and the people I've interacted with throughout the state for the past sixty-plus years.

My parents were both college graduates, which was unusual in the 1950s. My mother was a registered nurse. My father was a pharmacist. We moved to Fairmount, North Dakota, a community of five hundred people, before my brother Steve and I started school. Steve was fourteen months younger than I. Mike was born when I was seven and John arrived when I was eleven—quite an age gap; it was like two separate families with the same parents.

My dad operated a drugstore, and I started working there when I was eleven. At the beginning, I helped with inventory, wrapped gifts, and dusted shelves. Later, when I could add and subtract sufficiently, I got to use the ancient cash register and ring up sales.

My mother provided emergency services to anyone who needed medical care in our small town. She also agreed to be a private-duty nurse at the Breckenridge hospital, twenty-seven miles from Fairmount. She would spend the night with people who were dying.

I was exposed to many different cultures, even though I lived in North Dakota my entire life. The small community where we lived owned a house for doctors across the street from our house. The foreign doctors who took turns living in the house were hired to provide medical services to an underserved population. As a result, I grew up exposed to international foods like rice and curry (India). I knew how to use chopsticks before I started school (Korea) and had tasted borscht provided by the Jewish doctor who came from New York. My parents socialized with the doctors, and my siblings and I played with their kids.

Medicare changed the world for anyone working in a health care occupation in 1965, with the start of Lyndon Johnson's "Great Society" programs. That was the same year the current doctor in the small clinic ran off with his office nurse. The clinic closed, making the local drugstore obsolete. My parents had to find a new plan for work. Then, the furnace in our house exploded in March, and we lost everything in the fire that followed. With the drugstore closing and our house a total loss, it was time to move.

I learned about being homeless firsthand. I wore donated clothing for the rest of that school year. We were given a place to live by generous people in the community, so we weren't out on the streets. We were fortunate.

My family moved back to Wahpeton, North Dakota, in August 1965, where my dad took a job in a clinic pharmacy and my mother started working at the hospital in Breckenridge, Minnesota, part-time. I was a new kid in a much larger school, and I was starting high school. I've always said that being the new kid made me who I am today. As a result, I'm not afraid of meeting new people and I make friends easily. I still have close friends from high school who keep in touch.

My dad had me help him in the clinic pharmacy and treated me like the oldest son, much to Steve's chagrin. My dad always treated me like "one of the boys," and I did things like hunting and fishing with him and Steve. Dad couldn't wait for me to drive, so I could transport my little brothers where they needed to go and deliver prescriptions to homebound patients. As a result of that early driving experience, I'm good at finding addresses wherever I live or travel.

My mother treated me like Cinderella. She always worked the night shift (11:00 p.m. to 7:00 a.m.). Mom would see us off to school in the morning before she went to bed and get up before we got home from school. This worked well for her, but it was a problem for me, managing three young boys on weekends, holidays, and summers so she could sleep. My two younger brothers always said they had two "moms."

Liberation

I graduated from high school in 1970, and I couldn't wait to get away to college. I chose the University of North Dakota in Grand Forks, another city that shares a border with Minnesota. As it was over one hundred fifty miles from home and I didn't have a car, I didn't go home much, including the summers, while I was in college. I finally had some freedom from my family responsibilities.

The '70s both continued and escalated concepts and expressions of freedom and revolution. Some of the cultural influences that took place while I was in college (1970-1974) include the Kent State shootings, *Roe v. Wade* making abortion legal, the Equal Rights Amendment (ERA) failed, the Vietnam War entered its second decade, and both the US president and vice president resigned while in office. It was a volatile period in the United States. It also is remembered as a time of women's liberation and increased sexual freedom. For a small-town North Dakota female—even though living in a city—*that* revolution swirled around me.

I started dating Mike Gregory during my last year in college. Most of my friends dated his friends, and several of my friends eventually married his fraternity brothers. These relationships were like a big extended family. Mike and his brother Mark were members of the same fraternity at UND, as was Steve.

Oliver Gregory, Mike's dad, paid the brothers' expenses at college, gave them generous spending money, and provided nice cars for them to drive. In part, I believe Oliver thought that keeping his boys entertained at college was the best way to help them deal with their mother's death. Susan Gregory, who would have been my mother-in-law, died about the same time I started dating Mike, and indeed, the brothers partied a lot to deal with their grief. Their fraternity brothers liked to drink and have fun too, so it was like a never-ending party. Surprisingly, many of these college friends went on to successful careers as doctors, lawyers, and accountants!

The Vietnam War was still a threat to young men in college, and most couldn't visualize a future after the war ended. The Gregory brothers were fortunate to avoid the draft. I can still remember the night of the selective service drawing, when draft numbers were assigned. Mike and Mark, along with my brother Steve, all had high draft numbers, so they weren't drafted.

Several of our friends joined ROTC. They were hoping that if they had to serve, they could be officers. Luckily, we didn't lose any friends in Vietnam.

After college, I stayed in Grand Forks where I found a job in advertising, and then was transferred to Fargo in 1976, where I had more responsibilities with the same company.

Mike and I dated for seven years while he went back home and worked in his dad's car dealership in the small town of Cavalier. Mark worked there as well, so the brothers drove fancy cars, and they both lived in Oliver's house. The three Gregorys spent all day together at work and lived together too.

Mike and I saw each other on weekends and had a lot of fun with our mutual friends from college. Mike usually came to Fargo to see me, but when there were social activities in Cavalier, I would travel there for the weekend. That's where I originally met Jack Wahl in 1973. He was like a member of the Gregory family and was always included in their family activities. The first time I met Jack, I thought that he was such a nice, humble guy. I remember hearing about his art collection at that first meeting, although it was small compared to what he accumulated over the next ten-plus years. He was very easy to talk to, and I enjoyed him right away.

After graduating, I managed to support myself, even though jobs were hard to find—initially in Grand Forks, and then later in Fargo, where I was an advertising manager for a chain of regional men's stores. Those five years after college were wonderful for me. I only had to look out for myself. I drove a used car (a

1967 Mercury), and I shared rent with a roommate. I even had enough money to be able to travel with my girlfriends. By 1975, I was living like a career girl on *The Mary Tyler Moore Show*.

Eventually I enrolled in graduate courses at Moorhead State University (MSUM), wanting something more to do during the week. As a result of attending graduate school, I was asked to teach a couple of classes at the two-year technical college in Moorhead, Minnesota, so I was busy all week while Mike was in Cavalier. I never dated anyone else; I never met anyone who interested me. It was difficult to only see Mike on weekends, but I found things to do that I enjoyed.

I had completed the coursework for a master's degree in vocational education by 1979. All I had to do to get a teacher's certificate for North Dakota was student teach and revise my thesis. I was thinking about a future with Mike and living in Cavalier, so I was planning for life in a small town. I knew there wouldn't be jobs in advertising in Cavalier.

Mike liked to spend money and travel, and I was a beneficiary of this interest. I was able to travel with him every year leading up to our marriage, and then after we were married as well. We spent our honeymoon in Paris and the French Rivera. My dad once told me that he was jealous of our ability to travel.

2. About Cavalier

I'VE NAMED THIS BOOK *CAVALIER* after the small North Dakota town where I lived from 1979-1990. It is important to understand the rural area where my story is centered and the unique culture of living in a remote area, where winter demands that its people are independent and hardy, while they also are dependent on each other for social activities. Jack Wahl's unsolved murder owes much to the nature and dynamics of a small town.

The town of Cavalier is located in a remote, sparsely populated rural area where most of the longtime residents know one another. In fact, many of the citizens of Pembina County, where Cavalier is located, are related either by blood or through marriage. Someone explained to me that this was the result of the original homesteaders who didn't travel out of the area much in the early days.

Soon after arriving, I was warned to never speak badly about anyone in Pembina County, because they are probably related. Once, I was talking to a coworker who was recently divorced, and I suggested one of the local single men I knew as a potential date. She replied, "He is my cousin!"

Only someone like me, who has joined the community from "outside" the region, can appreciate what it's like to move to a small, rural community where everyone has known each other for generations. As I've said, I make friends easily, so I managed to bridge what others might have found challenging.

Where in the World is Cavalier?

The city of Cavalier isn't on the way to anywhere. When people have asked me where Cavalier is located, I've always said, "Take I-29 north and turn left just before you get to Canada." US Interstate Highway 29 begins in Texas and runs north to Winnipeg, Manitoba, but if you take North Dakota Exit 203, you will arrive in Cavalier after driving eighteen miles west on State Highway 5, a two-lane, farm-to-market road with no shoulders and deep ditches on either side.

Cavalier is the county seat for Pembina County, the oldest county in North Dakota. In the 1960s and 1970s, there were almost thirteen thousand residents living in Pembina County, due to the Cold War military buildup in the region. By the time I lived there, Cavalier numbered just fifteen hundred residents, and Pembina County was home to about ten thousand. Today, only twelve hundred reside in Cavalier and in the entire county, seventy-five hundred. Notably, there are forty-six county cemeteries—a testament to how many people have lived there since it was founded in 1867.

Pembina County shares its eastern border with Kittson County, Minnesota; to the south is Walsh County, North Dakota; and along its western border is Cavalier County, North Dakota. (Readers should not be confused by the existence of another nearby small town called Pembina, and the county of Cavalier, just thirty-five miles west of the town of Cavalier.) The largest nearby US city is Grand Forks, North Dakota, eighty-five miles to the south.

Almost a Canadian

I often told friends that "Cavalier was halfway between both (US) coasts." It is located near the center of the country, at its northern border. On the other side of that border is Manitoba, Canada—a separate province in a separate country. Winnipeg, Manitoba, is located one hour north of the US/Canadian border.

As many people live in Winnipeg as live in the entire state of North Dakota. When you live in a remote area like Cavalier, it is wonderful to have a large international city nearby to visit. There was certainly a Canadian influence on the region. We went to Winnipeg a lot, both while Mike and I were dating, and then later after we were married.

I wish I had paid more attention in French class, because we had both French-speaking and traditional English television and radio stations. Sometimes when I was flipping TV channels, I would see a popular American television show, like *Dallas*, totally in French! When I traveled in the US, people would often mistake me for a Canadian as a result of my accent, although I never said "eh" like real Canadians do.

Community Culture

One of the unique features of the city of Cavalier is the Tongue River, which winds its way through the community, creating small islands and peninsulas. There are no straight roads in Cavalier, making it unique for North Dakota, where most streets are arranged on a simple grid.

The river also helps to define the various neighborhoods with natural boundaries. A walking bridge connects the north and south parts of town. In the summer, south-side kids use the bridge to get to the swimming pool and park. In the fall, north-side students utilize the walking bridge to get to school.

Walking bridge, Cavalier, ND.

When I became familiar with the walking bridge, I led an initiative to replace it. It had been built by a city crew one winter in the 1950s, and it featured chicken-wire railings. The river had eroded the banks on both sides over the years, so there was an opening on each end that I felt was dangerous. I wanted my future children to be safe when they were old enough to utilize the bridge! It took me three years of work with the City Council, the local water board, and the Pembina County Commissioners to get approval for a new bridge and raise the money.

Pembina County

Thanks to ancient glaciers, the Pembina County region features rich, dark, black soil. In the spring and summer, when the crops are growing, the land is green as far as you can see, and you can see for a long distance because it is so flat! By fall, the fields are amber with the grain crops waiting for harvest, and when the current year's crops are harvested and hauled to local grain elevators, the ground returns to black—for a brief time before the snow falls.

During the winter season, which can last for more than six months, everything turns white from the relentless, blowing snow with the exception of the shelter belts (rows of trees planted by local farmers). The temperature is frequently below zero degrees Fahrenheit throughout the region. Coupled with the endless wind and frequent snowfall, there are many times that you can't leave town in the winter. You simply can't see to drive anywhere!

There isn't much industry other than farming in Pembina County with the exception of the sugar beet plant in Drayton, North Dakota, a farmer's co-op, and the bus manufacturing plant in Pembina. Many of the area farmers have become wealthy growing sugar beets that do well in that black soil. The bus plant is owned by a Canadian company, but employs many from the county, as well as from Kittson County, Minnesota.

The permanent, man-made dikes along each government boundary are the only elevations in the region. The Red River Valley is so flat that when the Red River floods, water spreads out for twenty miles in every direction. The altitude where the Red River begins in Wahpeton, North Dakota (my hometown, where I went to high school and where my parents lived for over fifty years), is 287 meters, or approximately 945 feet, above sea level. Lake Winnipeg is at 218 meters, or 715 feet above sea level, a decline of just 230 feet over 300 miles. Not surprisingly, flooding is an annual occurrence in the region for both the Americans and the Canadians—something that everyone in the area has in common.

Another commonality is that the population is mostly of Scandinavian descent and, thus, 95.5 percent Caucasian. Almost 20 percent of the population is over age sixty-five. Though not very diverse, Pembina County is home to the largest concentration of Icelandic people in the US, adding to its unique culture. Each year, the local Icelanders celebrate Iceland's Independence Day on August 2, and so does everyone else in the area.

I remember one of the area school superintendents saying that he had difficulty quantifying the diversity in his K-12 school system for a federal form. He decided to focus on the students with Icelandic heritage to demonstrate the school's diversity (you could tell by their last names). When someone from Washington,

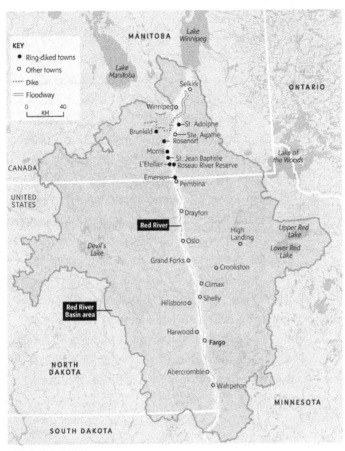

KEY

- Ring-diked towns
- Other towns
···· Dike
═══ Floodway

0 ————— 40
KM

MANITOBA · Lake Winnipeg · Lake Manitoba · Selkirk · Winnipeg · St. Adolphe · Ste. Agathe · Rosenort · Brunkild · Morris · St. Jean Baptiste · L'Etellier · Roseau River Reserve · Emerson · Pembina · ONTARIO · Lake of the Woods · CANADA · UNITED STATES · Red River · Drayton · Oslo · High Landing · Upper Red Lake · Lower Red Lake · Devil's Lake · Grand Forks · Crookston · Climax · Shelly · Red River Basin area · Hillsboro · Harwood · Fargo · NORTH DAKOTA · Abercrombie · Wahpeton · MINNESOTA · SOUTH DAKOTA

THE RED RIVER BASIN SLOPE

As the last glacier receded, the river actually flowed south; today,
it flows north across a flat plain, rich in topsoil left by a long-vanished lake. The flooding threat is made worse because
the river flows south to north, meaning the upper reaches thaw before the lower river.

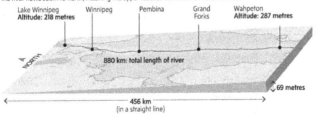

Lake Winnipeg
Altitude: 218 metres   Winnipeg   Pembina   Grand Forks   Wahpeton
Altitude: 287 metres

NORTH

880 km: total length of river

69 metres

←——————— 456 km ———————→
(in a straight line)

CARRIE COCKBURN/THE GLOBE AND MAIL
SOURCES: THE CANADIAN ENCYCLOPEDIA; MUSEEDUFJORD.COM; MANITOBA GOVERNMENT

The Red River Valley topography; Cavalier Chronicle.

DC, called to clarify, he explained, "Icelanders are kind of like Eskimos."

Pembina County also features residents of mixed decent called *Métis*. They have French-Canadian and Native American heritage and trace their origins to the early settlers and fur traders of the Red River Valley and Manitoba. These cultures make the area unique, since both the Icelandic and the *Metí* populations in the US are concentrated in this area.

Five miles west of Cavalier on State Highway 5 is the Renwick Dam and Icelandic State Park recreation area, with its man-made lake and nature preserve. The Pembina County Pioneer Heritage Center, highlighting the homestead era (1870-1920), adjoins the recreation area, the nine-hole community golf course, and a history museum. The town of Langdon, North Dakota, is due west on this route, a distance of thirty-five miles. It's located "next door" in Cavalier County, on the west side of the escarpment, or the sandy shore of the ancient glaciers.

Military Influence

North Dakota is a strategic location for the US military, with two large air force bases. In the seventies, there were many Minuteman missiles buried beneath the farmland, although they haven't been active for decades.

If you travel ten miles southwest of Cavalier, you'll see "Nixon's Pyramid," the radar tracking site for the entire northern border of North America.

Known initially as the Cavalier Air Force Station, the base is staffed by thirty military along with civilians from nearby towns. The base was renamed the Cavalier Space Force Station on July 30, 2021. It will become part of the new US Space Force Program.

The early days in the 1970s, building the Cavalier Air Force Station, now known as the Cavalier Space Force Station.

The base still contains a satellite tracking site operated by NORAD, or the North American Aerospace Defense Command.

During the Cold War in the 1970s, the construction of this base brought an extra ten thousand people to the region. It is still considered a *remote* tour of duty for the military. If you have seen the Netflix series *Designated Survivor*, you have seen a sample of what the area was like during that time period.

Air Force newcomers to Pembina County and Cavalier soon discovered the unique art techniques and artists who lived in this region, most of whom only created work for their families and friends at that time. With long winters indoors, the local artisans had plenty of time to paint china, master the art of Scandinavian rosemaling, and create needle crafts, including Hardanger embroidery. As the military newcomers (many of whom had lived all over the world) and the locals got to know each other, art shows and classes multiplied. Thus, by the time I moved to Cavalier, there was a thriving art culture and an annual regional art show.

Early Experiences

Cavalier and rural Pembina County are one of those regions where you don't need a turn signal on your car, because everyone knows your vehicle, and they know where you are headed! (There is no need for personalized license plates.) Even the UPS driver, who understood the relationships of the area, might stop to see if you'd take a package to your "neighbor" (and the driver lived in Grand Forks).

When my friends would come to visit, I knew that they truly made the effort to visit *me*, since there wasn't much else to see in the area. One sunny spring day, two of my college friends drove into Cavalier and stopped to get gas on their way to a marathon race in Winnipeg. At the gas station, they asked if someone could tell them where to find me. They were driving a red Porsche convertible, so by the time they arrived at my house, I'd received three phone calls telling me that there were two cute guys in a convertible coming to see me. That was what small-town life was like!

In 1978, Mike purchased a house before we married, which flooded in April 1979, before we moved in. I drove north on I-29 to get to Cavalier from Fargo to see the damage. There was water in every direction, as far as I could see. I was able to keep my car on the road by watching the mile markers that lined the pavement. It's one of the scariest situations I've ever encountered!

In May 1979, I was in Cavalier to decide what to do with our flooded house when Monsignor Lekavy, the priest at the local Catholic Church since 1951, heard I was in town and contacted Mike. The monsignor told him that we had to come and meet with him the next day, or he wouldn't approve our wedding. We made time for the appointment, even though I wasn't a Catholic and we weren't getting married in the Catholic Church. I had arranged to have my dad's uncle marry us in the local Methodist church in my hometown.

I really hadn't considered that I was moving to Mike's hometown—and because he was Catholic, the community expected that I would be Catholic too. People didn't change religions often in those days, and I had no interest in becoming a Catholic, but there was social pressure to make that change. Just to put religion in perspective, there were over forty churches in Pembina County, eight of those located in Cavalier. I was a Methodist, and there were two Methodist churches in Cavalier for just fifteen hundred total residents! A religious identity was important in a small town.

I had never met Msgr. Lekavy, a former World War II prisoner of war from Czechoslovakia, but his reputation preceded him. It seems that in Czechoslovakia a priest is treated almost like a king in the community where he "reigns." The monsignor still expected automatic respect from his "subjects," whether they were Catholic or not.

Mike wasn't very religious, so I was surprised that he succumbed to the monsignor's requirements. We had to take compatibility tests during that first visit with Monsignor Lekavy. When our goals aligned, he accused Mike and me of collaborating on the test, even though we had completed our compatibility tests in separate rooms. He made us retake the test. This was a great first impression for me!

As we were leaving the rectory after the second test, Msgr. Lekavy asked who could vouch for me. He didn't believe that I, at age twenty-seven, hadn't been married previously. I told him both Jim Salaba and Jack Wahl had both known me since 1973. He promised to verify those local references.

Engagement party Kathleen Nessheim hosted— Kathleen, Jack, me, and Mike.

Serendipitously, a college friend of ours was in the seminary. His summer job that year included visiting each parish in the diocese and meeting the local priests. When our friend Father Tim stopped by to meet Msgr. Lekavy the day after we had completed our compatibility tests, he mentioned that he knew both Mike and me.

Later that day, Monsignor Lekavy called us and said, "It's providence! Father Tim has vouched for you." And that's all it took. We had the local Catholic Church's approval to get married—with one more hoop to jump through.

Due to the region-wide flooding that spring, all of the mandatory premarital counseling events had been canceled by the Catholic Church. The make-up class was to be held in Grand Forks in late May. When we arrived at the church, the line of brides and grooms circled the entire block. Every couple in the diocese getting married that summer was required to attend the weekend marriage counseling session by each of their local churches.

After standing in line for over an hour, we finally reached the reservation table. Three ancient church ladies staffed the check-in desk. We gave them our names and were told, "Monsignor Lekavy left a note. He said that you were rich and that you should pay double tuition."

Monsignor Lekavy was also famous for publishing an annual "list of shame," where he listed each family's donations to the church for the previous twelve months. As you might expect, this was controversial in a small town where everyone knew each other.

Since the Gregorys were Catholic, we attended the local church periodically after we were married. I eventually represented the family by working with Monsignor Lekavy on a variety of projects, including remodeling the church and building a new rectory. I wasn't really a volunteer. Instead, I was told that I would be working with the monsignor by the Gregory family. I was their contribution to the local church, I guess!

As I got to know Monsignor Lekavy, he told me that he was like a "nomadic stone." I later learned that he meant that he was moved around like the rocks you found in the area farm fields that had been pushed from place to place by the early glaciers. It was difficult to see his perspective. To me, he was the "pusher"!

3. The First Year in Cavalier

Married

MIKE HAD PURCHASED A HOUSE one block from his
dad's new house the year prior to our wedding,
though he continued to live with his dad and brother.
His bedroom was on the basement level, which flooded in April 1979. After that, he moved into our house,
which also had river water in the basement, but the
main floor was dry. No water pumps were available
anywhere in the region that spring, since the entire
Red River Valley was flooded, so the river water just sat
in both houses. When we married that June, three feet
of river water still filled our basement, and it was still
there when we returned from our honeymoon in July.

Our wedding took place in Wahpeton, on June 16,
1979. Monsignor Lekavy made sure that there was a
priest present, or our marriage wouldn't be "recognized" without a priest in attendance. Since I wasn't
Catholic, I didn't understand any of this reasoning,
but I went along with it to appease the Gregory family.

My dad's uncle, a Methodist pastor, conducted the
service with a "pirate" patch over one eye. (I guess he

had emergency eye surgery the previous week and was told by his physician that he had to wear it 24/7.) His appearance seemed fitting for the wild party that ensued at the local Elks Club to celebrate our wedding and added mystery to the wedding photos!

Our college friends attended the wedding and serenaded us with the "Sigma Chi Sweetheart" song, a tradition for Mike's fraternity brothers. Two of my sorority sisters were bridesmaids. My brother Steve, who was a fraternity brother with Mike and Mark Gregory, refused to be an usher and wear a tux, so instead he wore a yellow suit and sat in the audience at the church. He was in dental school at the time.

Oliver, Mike's dad, was a known womanizer, by the time we married. (His wife, Susan, had been dead for eight years.) As a wealthy widower in a small community, Oliver was in big demand. He had many girlfriends, so you never knew who might show up as his date. Three of his girlfriends attended our wedding, each of them vying for attention in their low-cut dresses and fancy hats. My mother didn't know what to do with them! She didn't drink much, and she would have never worn a dress that showed cleavage. She spent part of the wedding reception breaking up the girlfriends' disputes. Meanwhile, Oliver was just having a good time!

We honeymooned in France, and our friend Jack came to our house regularly and poured disinfectant everywhere in the flooded basement, to avoid mold. Jack was building a new home a block from our house and next door to Oliver, but it was in the early framing stages, so his house didn't need much of his attention.

After we settled in, Mike continued to go to work each day, leaving me alone that summer to deal with the workmen who were rebuilding our basement rooms. I was frustrated with the project, since Mike had made several decisions without my input. For example, he had the opportunity to redo the floor plan, since the entire space was demolished, but he didn't make any changes. He also made the decision to finish the walls with wood paneling. I would have chosen sheet rock and textured the walls.

I was painting the living room in September when the three Gregorys stopped by to tell me that the book-keeper at the car dealership had quit, and that I was going to take her job.

I said, "No. I'm going to revise my thesis, and then I'm going to student teach and get a teaching job."

Oliver wouldn't take no for an answer, and the following week I went to work in the family business. Now I was spending all day with Mike, his brother, and his dad. I always described the Gregorys as having a "split personality." Mike, Mark, and Oliver each had a third, and together they were a whole person! Three against one—and I was female. I didn't stand a chance. (It was like being married to three people at once, since all decisions were made by the *troika*.) This wasn't how I pictured my small-town life would be.

I quickly learned that Mike's dad would make decisions that most newly married couples usually worked out together. After all, he controlled the money Mike earned, the cars we drove, and eventually our home, since he paid off our mortgage. It didn't take long to see that Mike only did what Oliver wanted him to do. I never had a vote.

Nor did Mike do any work around the house. We always hired people for the chores that most home-owners do themselves. It's also a fact that he never did much at work at the dealership, either, thanks to his dad owning the business. Mike's job description was salesman, but most of the customers, many of them wealthy farmers, would order a new car or pickup every year, so Mike just had to wait for them to appear at the dealership.

Not to trash poor Mike, but he never did anything to excess, except eat and drink too much. And if there was an emergency at work and no one else around to drive the wrecker, he didn't even know how to start it. He kept his friends on "speed dial" in his office and spent a lot of time talking with them every day to pass the time.

Susan

The family's story of my mother-in-law's death in 1971 was that she slipped and fell in the bathtub. Dr. Jack Wahl was a family friend and the Pembina County Coroner, so it wasn't much of a stretch to think that he would document the cause of Susan's death according to Oliver's account of the accident. While Susan's friends in the community accepted the bathtub story, they nevertheless questioned it. Her close friends knew she had been depressed and assumed that she committed suicide. But she was able to have a church funeral, and that was important to the family and her friends, since she was a devout Catholic and participated in daily mass.

Susan had reason to be depressed. Her son John had died in her arms, at age seven, of congenital heart disease. This happened while they were on the way to the Mayo Clinic in Rochester, Minnesota. And her son James, eighteen months younger than John, had been diagnosed as mentally retarded. (No one used the terms *mentally challenged* or *cognitively impaired* in those days.) Susan also had her hands full with two teenage sons who were soon leaving for college. By the time I started dating Mike, the eldest of the four boys, James was living in a foster care home under the care of one of Oliver's girlfriends. As a widower with a business to run, he couldn't manage James too.

Susan Gregory had been known in the small community as a prolific artist. No one knew when she had time to paint as the mother of four young boys, but she painted a lot. Perhaps it was her therapy? She painted in oils and acrylics and finished her art with a collection of antique picture frames that she purchased from area estate sales and auctions.

Years later, my daughter and I took one of Susan's paintings to have it reframed. The clerk in the art store was amazed at the quality of Susan's work, since there were few art classes available during the 1960s when she painted. The painting was signed with Susan's name, and the date, 1966.

Jack Wahl and Susan Gregory often discussed antiques and frequented estate sales together. They shared a love of art. I never met Susan, but local people often remarked that Jack and I had a similar relationship. I enjoyed the same things that were the foundation of Jack and Susan's relationship, so it was an instant friendship for Jack and me when I moved to Cavalier. From my perspective, I had three brothers and Jack had three sisters, so it was very much like hanging out with another brother.

Susan's husband, Oliver, was a workaholic with a classic car salesman's personality. You could only believe about half of what he said, but he did well in the car business and was very social. He was also very controlling of Susan's time, according to family friends. For example, he would come home several times during the day for coffee, snacks, and meals. As a result, Susan could never make plans to see her friends. She did get time off to attend church every morning, though.

Oliver

My father-in-law was sometimes hard to take, especially when he had been drinking. He liked to party a lot, and when he had too much to drink, he often said hurtful things to me, regardless of who was nearby to overhear it. One night at a gathering, not long after I'd moved to Cavalier, Oliver said to me in front of a group, "You wish I was dead, don't you?"

Why did he have to be so confrontational in public? Encounters like this did make me imagine how much easier life would be without Oliver in the picture, though I would imagine him retiring and moving out of town—not dying. I was upset, so I left Mike at the party, took one of the family cars, and went home.

Most of the locals left their keys in their cars, and many of them left them in the ignition. The Gregorys *always* left the keys in their cars in Cavalier, because every vehicle the Gregory family members drove was for sale, and one of them might need to show it to a customer. I knew that someone would eventually come for the car, and Oliver would have to drive by our house to get to his home, so they would see the car in the driveway and know that the car was safe at least!

Grandma Sadie

Oliver won many sales contests and as a result, he and Susan were able to travel the world. During those vacations, Oliver's mother, Sadie, would stay with the boys. The Gregory brothers had a good relationship with their Grandma Sadie. She was quite a character!

Sadie had raised two boys of her own and worked in a bar with her husband. She could hold her ground in a "man's world." Sadie enjoyed swearing and drinking brandy at night. She called her drink a "hog" shot. When her brandy ran low, she liked to accuse the family of drinking her booze! She famously stated that she never started dinner until she could see "the whites of their eyes," because her son, and later her grandsons, would often stop for drinks on their way home from work.

I enjoyed Grandma Sadie and her friends. All of them were opinionated, so you didn't have to wonder what they were thinking! They told stories of when they had been my age (two generations previous) and about hard work and life during World War II when they raised their families. They all worked outside their homes at low-paying jobs in the community. In those days, women's needs were not well supported, and these ladies were much more dependent on their spouses than I was. I remember thinking that I was lucky to have an education, and I already knew I could support myself.

Sadie's husband, Oliver Sr., died in 1967, just as they began celebrating retirement. Her son Oliver taught Sadie how to drive a car after his dad died, so that she could be independent. She lived approximately one hundred miles from Cavalier, and there was no public transportation. There are many stories of her initial driving experiences, including the one where "the dash lit up like high mass!" She had blown up the engine on that car.

Small Town Nuances

The Gregorys were a very tight knit group! Mike, Mark, and Oliver spent all day together at the car dealership from 8:00 a.m. until 9:00 p.m., Monday through Saturday. Mark still lived with Oliver, so after work Mike usually joined them at his dad's house. That first year, I was alone a lot.

Another small-town nuance that I had to learn involved the postal service. The Gregorys had one mail box that they shared at the local post office. The car dealership received mail at P.O. Box 340, as did Grandma Sadie, and now me. When I started working at the dealership, I discovered that all my magazines were in the waiting room. Mike never brought them home. (And I just thought that the address changes I had made before I left Fargo weren't working!) In addition, the Cavalier post office closed from 12:30-1:30 so the workers could watch *Days of Our Lives*. This wasn't very customer-friendly for working people who wanted to stop for their mail over their lunch hour, but the locals all just seemed to accept this reality. I also learned to accept that films shown at the local movie theater would sometimes just quit in the middle, and we wouldn't get to see the ending.

Everyone in Cavalier was friendly. At first of course, I didn't know anyone, but they sure knew me—I was *not* a native. It wasn't unusual to have people walk up to me and say things like, "You're not from here, are you?" or "Now, who are you?" Another time as Mike and I entered Sammy's Bar, someone yelled from the back of the bar, "Hey, Connie. Where did you come from? We have a bet going—Fargo or Grand Forks?" I smiled at the strangers and said, "You're both right. I have lived in Fargo *and* Grand Forks."

4. Jack Wahl

Jack's House

OLIVER GREGORY, DR. JACK WAHL, and Dr. Jamil (Jim) Tareen, the local surgeon, had purchased four river lots in the late 1970s, planning to build three homes, the largest in the community. The back yards of the houses came together on pie-shaped lots, and the Tongue River ran behind them. The two doctors previously lived next door to each other on the west end of town. They were also partners in the medical clinic and good friends.

Oliver's house was completed in 1978, and the other two took a couple of years longer. Jack's home was in the middle, with Dr. Tareen's house on the north side and Oliver's just to the east. Jack began construction on his house shortly before my arrival in 1979. Once all three were built, they sat at such angles to one another that it was impossible to see from one house to the other. And due to the elevation of the land, the rest of the houses on the street weren't visible.

The three houses all had walkout basements, so they looked like two-story homes from the back yard. Each featured a main-level garage, with storage space underneath and decks that ran the entire length of the structure.

My father-in-law's new home also flooded in April 1979. I remember that the sliding glass doors of the basement made it look like an aquarium, except that it featured dirty river water and tree branches instead of goldfish. The flooded storeroom under the garage was filled with antique furniture and furnishings from Oliver's former house, things that Susan had accumulated. Most were ruined now. At one point, Jack and I were walking around my father-in-law's basement in waders, trying to rescue whatever we could, when an Irish Belleek cup floated by. Jack grabbed it and just about had a heart attack! He knew a lot about collectibles, including dishes.

All three of the property owners were good friends and regularly had drinks and dinner together, until Oliver moved to Grand Forks in December 1983. One spring day, Jack saw Oliver out in his back yard. Jack grabbed his stethoscope and blood pressure cuff and walked next door. He took Oliver's vitals outside in the adjoining yard, because he hadn't seen Oliver for a while, and just wanted to check on how he was doing.

Most people in Cavalier didn't use their front doors. Jack entered his house through the side door to the oversized double garage. I don't ever remember an occasion when his front door was used. The side door was never locked. In fact, his *Grand Forks Herald* newspaper was delivered inside the garage door each day.

An exterior door on the back side of Jack's garage faced Oliver's home. This door was accessed via the

Jack's house.

wooden deck along the back of the house. Anyone could access the deck directly from the garage or the front of the house. Several sliding glass doors opened onto the long deck, including one on the main level from the master bedroom and one from the family room in the basement.

A large workroom was unfinished under Jack's garage, with an exterior door to the back yard. This workroom was primarily utilized by an artisan and friend of Jack's named Sally. She used the space to work on stained glass windows. If Jack had a project he was refinishing, he used this space too. I'm not sure if Sally had a key, or if the door was simply left unlocked.

There was an open kitchen and den when you entered through the garage. I remember that his kitchen table was always piled a foot high with mail and magazines. Near the kitchen, there was a half bath, the laundry room, and a greenhouse that faced the front of the house and the street. A small formal dining room adjoined the kitchen.

One night we grilled steaks in the wood-burning fireplace in the den. Another fireplace opened into the living room. Jack rarely used the living room, but the week prior to his murder, Dr. Maxine Rasmussen, a psychologist from Grand Forks, and I had drinks with Jack and sat in the living room. We talked about repurposing the room because it wasn't used much.

The main floor also included a large master bedroom with a huge master bath featuring a tub the size of a small swimming pool. It was probably twelve feet by ten feet, but it was shallow, not deep like a hot tub. When the house was being built, Jack said that he was putting in the large bathtub so Kari's little girl could swim. Kari and Jack were married for only one year, and unfortunately, Kari and her daughter never lived in the house. There was also a guest room and an office across the hall from the master bedroom.

A comfortable family room, the main entertaining space, was downstairs, with a large u-shaped sectional couch, big-screen television, restored antique bar with built-in glass cupboards, and shelves for his Roseville (Ohio) and Rosemead (Wahpeton) pottery collections. There was another guest bedroom downstairs too.

Jack's house was designed with high, raftered ceilings to showcase his art collection. Some of the art was large and occupied entire walls. It was like he lived in an art gallery.

A Friend for Me

Our friend Jack was always included in the Gregory family events, including birthdays and holidays. We were celebrating someone's birthday one night after work at our house. I had made dinner for the group and, of course, birthday cake. Grandma Sadie, who was now living with Oliver, joined us for dinner. At one point during the meal she suddenly said, "What the hell is wrong with these carrots? They taste like shit."

Jack politely responded, "They are candied carrots." Jack often came to my rescue at family dinners. In fact, he was the only one who ever defended me.

The other Gregorys simply said, "They do" (taste like shit).

Another time, at Jack's house eating dinner, Oliver said something ridiculous, and I responded with what I thought was a sensible explanation. Oliver went on a

Grandma Sadie and Jack Wahl at our house, 1979.

rant, saying, "What the hell do you know about it?" In general, he didn't believe that women knew anything about anything.

Jack calmly grabbed my hand that night and said, "It's okay. They're crazy. You are not." There have been so many times over the years that I have had to recall Jack defending me. To keep my sanity, I learned to tell myself, "They're crazy, I'm not."

Jack's Background

Jack Wahl grew up in Hannaford, a small town near the middle of North Dakota, so he knew what small-town life was like. He moved to Cavalier in 1969 after finishing medical school, at a time when Pembina County was considered a medically underserved area. Jack was recruited to work in the small-town clinic and thus avoided military service. (The Vietnam War was still raging.) He completed his undergrad studies at Concordia College in Moorhead, Minnesota, and attended medical school at UND, Grand Forks, with his primary care residency taking place at the University of Nebraska in Omaha.

Most of Jack's siblings and cousins also attended or graduated from Concordia College in Moorhead, so there was a strong connection to both Moorhead and Concordia for Jack. He wore his Concordia ring proudly. His cousins from Moorhead often visited Cavalier. Jack talked about them frequently and enjoyed a good relationship with each of his Benson relatives.

Jack was approximately six feet tall and had straight, light-brown hair. I would describe him as a little chubby. He didn't exercise at all. At work, he primarily wore scrubs and a lab jacket. After hours, he was usually dressed casually in a button down shirt and slacks, often covered with a lightweight sweater or jacket because he was often cold. Although he owned nice suits and ties, there were infrequent reasons for him to dress formally. He was a casual guy.

Mike, Grandma Sadie, Jack, Mark, and Oliver.

In the 1980s, it was still socially acceptable to smoke, and Jack smoked anywhere he wanted, including in the hospital, at the nursing home, and in the clinic. In those days, you didn't have to leave the building to have a cigarette. Anyone could smoke in restaurants and bars too. I remember that Jack was even smoking a cigarette the first time he brought my son, "Baby Jack," into my hospital room to meet me!

Jack enjoyed his income by traveling, driving luxury cars, and buying art from regional artists. Sometimes he would drive a Lincoln purchased from my in-laws, and other years he would drive a Cadillac from Page's. Both dealerships were located in Cavalier and both of the car dealers were his friends. He wanted to be fair to everyone, so he took turns buying cars from his friends. Jack was like that.

Jack had friends of all ages. He especially loved his older patients, because "they had such interesting stories to tell." When he would make rounds at the local nursing home, he spent time asking the residents about their families. Each resident felt that he took a personal interest in them, and he did. Some of the residents would dress up or get their hair done before he was scheduled to visit.

Jack often talked about his paternal grandfather, the only grandfather he knew. He would credit his grandfather for leaving him an inheritance, although he didn't have access to the funds until he was thirty-five. Sometimes, when we were out socializing or traveling, Jack would buy a special bottle of wine. He liked Pouilly Fuissé, a white wine. I still buy this wine for special occasions, and I think of Jack when I do. Other times, Jack might pay for dinner, toasting his benefactor by saying, "Thanks, Grandfather!" The relationship with Jack's grandfather established the foundation of his love for the elderly, which Jack was able to incorporate into his medical practice. He was also close with his uncle Arvid, who became Jack's financial advisor.

Jack got along naturally with older generations, and he formed a special relationship with Grandma Sadie, who lived next door with Oliver. She had a stroke about the time Oliver moved into his new home, and Sadie soon moved in too. Living next door, Jack visited frequently to check on her. When Sadie could no longer live at home and needed nursing home care, Jack was the one who broke the news to her and convinced her that she needed skilled nursing care. She listened to Jack, but no one in the family would have ever talked with her about her failing health. The Gregory guys were never very good at talking about anything negative. In fact, they avoided difficult discussions at all costs.

A couple of years later, I was working at the new nursing home, seven months pregnant with my son, Jack, when Grandma Sadie had a heart attack. The nursing home was located one mile from the hospital. I had just arrived for work, so I followed the ambulance to the hospital. Jack Wahl was already at the ICU when I arrived. He must have left the clinic as soon as the ambulance call was received.

When I arrived at the ICU, my first question to Jack was, "What about the baby?" He told me that Grandma Sadie wouldn't be around when the baby arrived in May.

He was with our family most of that day and later through the days leading up to the funeral. He was truly like a member of the family. Jack had similar relationships with many of the local families.

Kari

Jack married Kari in 1978. Their marriage didn't last long. Kari was a native of Norway who had a small daughter from a previous relationship. The marriage broke up about the same time Jack's new house was completed, and Kari returned to Norway. Prior to her departure, she told anyone who would listen that she was leaving because Jack was gay. Jack told everyone that Kari didn't like his friends.

I always thought of Jack as *asexual*, not interested in a sexual relationship with anyone. I've learned that asexuality is on a spectrum. It is not a choice. A person who has no sexual feelings or desires may simply have a low libido or sex drive. An asexual person can be emotionally invested in a relationship but not physically. However, some of the locals believed Jack lived a double life and that he was homosexual, especially after Kari announced the reason for her departure. The local community decided that she must be right, since after all she was married to Jack. To be fair, during the years that I lived in Cavalier, I heard that gay husbands were the foundation of many divorces.

Jack's uncle talked about Kari and Jack's marriage in an interview with the *Grand Forks Herald*, saying, "Kari and Jack knew each other for seven years prior to their marriage, but living in a small town was difficult, and then there were the cultural differences."[2]

Jack's cousin Mike added that Kari's mother had a heart attack during her first visit and was hospitalized in Cavalier. Relatives from Norway stayed with the couple for several weeks during her recuperation, and that added stress to the new marriage.

Once Kari was gone, I became the unofficial hostess for many of Jack's social events. We would spend a lot of time talking about who was or wasn't to be included on guest lists for various gatherings, including a big Fourth of July party that he hosted every year. As a result of these conversations, I knew who Jack liked and who he didn't.

Jack's Uncle Arvid provided the fireworks for the annual celebration from his furniture and appliance store in Moorhead. It was the biggest event in the community, and everyone wanted an invitation. Two individuals who were never included on the guest list were Neil Fleming, a local attorney and president of the hospital board, and Dr. David Watkin, one of Jack's physician partners in the Cavalier Clinic.

Traveling

We often traveled with Jack. One year, Jack, Mike, and I, along with friends Jim Salaba, and Claudia and Arnie Peterson, went to New York City between Thanksgiving and Christmas. We enjoyed plays, ate well, and shopped at Gucci and Steuben Glass.

These trips bolster my opinion that Jack was more asexual rather than homosexual. If I was gay and living

Our group on our way to New York City, 1984.

in a small town, I would utilize out-of-town trips to live out my gay life, but Jack never left our group when we traveled together. In fact, on the NYC trip, he paid for a limousine, so the group was together all the time. Jack didn't pay for everything, though. We each put money in a pool and paid for drinks and food from the group fund.

I remember going to the Steuben Glass store with Jack. It was very exciting, since he often brought me Steuben Glass from his travels. I still have a collection of those gifts. (I assumed that he bought gifts like this for all of his close friends.) At the store, he told me to pick out my next gift, and I chose the French Hen, which I still display in my home and think of that magical day in New York with good friends.

Over the years, Jack also gave me the serving pieces for the Lenox Christmas china that I wanted to collect, and frequently gave me Waterford Crystal presents. He liked to say that wine tasted better out of my Waterford goblets.

One time, we were in Minneapolis for an event. I remember getting into an elevator downtown where we had gone for dinner. A passenger on the elevator said, "Hello, doctor." (It was someone from North Dakota, whom I didn't know.) Even that far from home, people knew Jack!

5. The Art Community

THERE WERE SOME EARLY ART influencers in Jack's family. His grandmother gave lessons in china painting in the 1920s and painted watercolors until she was in her eighties. A still-life painted by his grandmother, Mable Cora Larson, was bequeathed to Jack when she died. His aunt Patty, who was married to Jack's mother's twin brother, supported art museums in the Fargo-Moorhead area where she lived and also purchased paintings from local artists for her home.

Jack initially became interested in collecting art during his undergraduate years at Concordia College (1960-1964). He often dropped by the new Rourke Gallery in Moorhead to look at art, and he eventually developed a friendship with Jim O'Rourke—who also attended Concordia at the time—and his brother, Orland Rourke (Jim added the O' in his surname). Jack became one of the founding members of the Rourke Gallery in 1973 when the organization moved to the old Moorhead post office building.

The Plains Art Museum eventually moved to Fargo, and Jack was named to its board of directors in 1975. He regularly loaned art from his growing collection to both galleries for shows. Jack also hung some of his art with the local bank in Cavalier, where he was an investor and served on the board of directors. Cavalier didn't have an art gallery, so this was Jack's way of sharing his art.

Jack was a frequent dinner guest at our house, and the bare walls bothered him! By 1986, we had eleven of Jack's paintings displayed in our home. He had chosen each painting for the space where it hung. He was always very generous with his art, as well as his time and his money throughout the community, and I'm sure other Cavalier friends benefited from sharing Jack's art collection too.

Jack's Art Collection

Jack's first art purchase, in 1972, was a painting named "Near Casselton." It was a small oil painting by Cyrus Running that Jack purchased from the Rourke Gallery. Originally from South Dakota, Cyrus Running was the Chairman of the Art Department at Concordia College from 1940–1974, so he was still working at Concordia when Jack was enrolled.

Running was well-known for designing the large murals featured at the annual Concordia Christmas Concert. Eventually, the art gallery at Concordia was named for him. Running was married and had four children. He died on Christmas Day 1976, but his influence on regional artists carries on his spirit of teaching to this day. A recent newspaper report describes Running's influence on James O'Rourke—and other regional artists.[2]

Another one of the artists featured in Jack's home was Cameron Booth, a Minnesota artist who painted abstracts, farm scenes, and animals. A painting called "Viaduct Pertaining to Washington Avenue Bridge" (1930), hung above the fireplace in Jack's formal living room.[3] Jack liked to point out to visitors that the delivery truck in the painting only had one headlight. The Whitney Museum in New York had offered to purchase a different Booth painting called "Crossing," but Jack wouldn't part with it.

Each painting in Jack's collection seemed to have a backstory, and Jack enjoyed educating his visitors and friends on the various artists' personal stories, since he actually knew them through Jim O'Rourke. Over time, Jack accumulated one of the largest collections of Midwest artists, including paintings by Cameron Booth, James Rosenquist, Gordon Mortensen, George Pfeifer, Cyrus Running, Jack Youngquist, and thirty to forty paintings and wood cuttings created by his friend and Moorhead artist, James O'Rourke. Some of these artists were Jack's contemporaries.

Each of the artists in Jack's collection had a Midwest connection. James Rosenquist had been a student of Cameron Booth at the University of Minnesota. Rosenquist was born in Grand Forks, North Dakota, in 1933, and became well known as an artist in New York, where he supported himself as a commercial sign painter. In the 1960s, he took his interest in pop art and combined it with his experience painting billboards, and he was forever known for his unusual and oversized paintings. Rosenquist had been commissioned to paint a large painting for the Plains Art Museum in Fargo, when a fire gutted his Florida home and studio. Eventually, he started over and his large painting now greets visitors when they arrive at the Plains Art Museum. James Rosenquist was married twice and died in 2017.

Gordon Mortensen was a woodcut artist, who was born in a very small town located in North Dakota called Arnegard.

George Pfeifer was born in Fargo in 1946 and is famous for his Midwest landscapes. He had his first solo exhibit at the Rourke Gallery in 1966. The painting we received as a wedding gift from Jack in 1979 was painted by Pfeifer. He currently lives in St. Paul, Minnesota, with his wife, Sharon.

This is the painting that we received as a wedding gift in 1979.

Jack Youngquist was a drawing instructor at Minnesota State University, located in Moorhead just a few blocks from Concordia College. Youngquist was another artist who was prominently featured in my friend's art collection and at the Rourke Gallery, which published a retrospective of his work in 1983.

Friends often celebrated these regional artists with Jack. I remember attending a memorial event at Jack's house when artist Cameron Booth died in 1980. Jack's collection, of course, grew in value when an artist died.

Jack supported local Cavalier and Pembina County artists too. Harriet Sampson was one of the talented local watercolorists who lived in the neighborhood between Jack's house and ours. She always contributed her paintings to the annual Cavalier Art Show. Jack was a huge fan of Harriet's art, and since he was a well-known collector, Harriet would invite him to see her paintings prior to the art show. He often brought me with him on these visits. As a result, I have several Harriet Sampson paintings in my home today. Harriet and her husband, Johnnie, were unfortunately killed in a car accident after I moved from Cavalier. I have never had her paintings appraised, but I still enjoy them to this day.

Fritz Scholder

Jack had given us a framed and signed poster ("to Connie & Mike") from a Fritz Scholder exhibit at the Rourke Gallery. Recently I saw the same poster, called "The Kat Show," which featured the "Portrait of a Cat, #1" (1979) by Fritz Scholder on an online website for over $800. I wish I had kept it! (I gave it to my nephew, who loved cats, when I left Cavalier.)

Since the day I received that poster, I have followed Fritz Scholder. I later learned that he was born in the same hospital where I was born, in Breckenridge, Minnesota. His father was employed by the Wahpeton Indian Boarding School as a school administrator, located in my hometown. Scholder was an enrolled member of the Luiseno tribe through his father. He also was a member of the California Mission tribe, but he did not consider himself to be Native American.

As part of my research for this book, I quickly learned that Fritz Scholder and Jim O'Rourke crossed paths in the Midwest "art world" many times. According to the Rourke Gallery's website, over thirty paintings by Scholder are included in the gallery's permanent collection. In addition, one of Scholder's five honorary degrees was awarded to him by Concordia College.

Imagine my surprise when I retired to Santa Fe in 2018 and saw Fritz Scholder's name and work everywhere in New Mexico. The artist and teacher definitely left his mark in Santa Fe, where he once taught art at the Institute of American Indian Arts (IAIA). Although I never met the artist, I have "crossed paths" with him several times now. I wouldn't have known of him at all if it wasn't for my friend Jack, the art collector who educated me.

Fritz Scholder died in 2005 following a well-documented career where he was known as an American Indian artist.

The Rourke Gallery

After launching the Rourke Gallery in 1960, artist and curator Jim O'Rourke and his brother Orland Rourke sponsored an annual art show in Moorhead, known as the Midwestern Art Exhibit. This annual event, which always opened on June 18, celebrated its sixtieth anniversary in 2019. This event provided important connections between the regional artists and local art collectors, and also an opportunity for Jack to get to know the artists personally.

I was often included when Jim O'Rourke came to Cavalier to pick up or return Jack's art from an exhibit. Sometimes this occurred late at night, since Jim had to drive three hours to get to Cavalier after his gallery closed for the day. We'd have a few drinks at Jack's house and talk about news from the "art world." I always enjoyed those late-night visits. Jim still had family in nearby Langdon, North Dakota, and would often include a visit there on his trips to Cavalier.

Jim had also been to our house with Jack, and he knew that one of the large pieces that hung on our red stairwell wall was one he had painted in 1966 while he was stationed in Europe. I remember that he thought my red wall provided the perfect background for his painting. This painting was eventually gifted to the North Dakota Museum of Art located on the UND campus and then sold by the museum in 2011 to an art enthusiast from Cooperstown, North Dakota.

6. The Health Care Community

The Doctors and the Clinic

WHEN DR. JACK WAHL JOINED the Cavalier Clinic, the community was served only by this small operation. It gradually grew and increased its services, staffed by four MDs and a general surgeon, who were equal partners in the business. Dr. E. J. Larson came to Cavalier from Canada in 1959 and was already living in Cavalier when the clinic was built in 1960. Dr. Jack Wahl joined the practice in 1969. A general surgeon, Dr. Jamil Tareen, joined the clinic in 1974, via Pakistan, Great Britain, and Winnipeg, Manitoba. Dr. David Watkin came in 1976, and Dr. Warren Jensen, a "hometown boy," joined the clinic in 1984.

The clinic and the hospital, along with an ambulance garage, were all located together on the east side of town. The hospital had been built with federal Hill-Burton funds and opened in 1951. By 1973, it had been expanded several times, and now included an indoor connection to the clinic. The hospital was owned by the community and featured local board members who represented each part of Pembina County. None of them had a medical background, so the hospital had been operated by a Fargo-based management company, Lutheran Hospitals and Homes Society, since it opened in 1951. Jack Wahl was the physician's representative to the local board.

The five physicians had a meeting room at the hospital where they had lunch together every day. Some of them, but not all of them, also got together after work to socialize. Both Dr. Wahl and Dr. Larson had Wednesday as their day off. Most Wednesdays, the two physicians would have dinner together at the Cedar Inn. Dr. Larson's wife, Pat, usually accompanied them. By the end of an evening, anyone else who was also dining at the Cedar Inn likely had joined them for drinks. It was common to see the small tables in the bar all pushed together in a group for these conversations, which included individuals from all walks of life and age groups.

The Hospital and Nursing Home

In January 1980, a new nursing home opened on the west side of Cavalier. The nursing home was funded by the local hospital board and managed by Lutheran Hospitals and Homes Society, just like the hospital. The hospital administrator asked me to join the hospital/nursing home staff. It was part-time work at the beginning. She told me that since she was trained as a nurse, she didn't have a marketing background. She had plans for a home health program, a walk-in clinic, and an assisted living building, and she needed my help.

For a while, I continued to work at the family car dealership too. When my hours increased at the nursing home, I was able to "give notice" at the garage—gladly. I was tired of spending every day with Mike, his dad, and his brother. I told people that it was easier to quit than to schedule therapy!

Over the eleven years I worked for the hospital and nursing home, I was responsible for fundraising, grant writing, social services, marketing, planning, public relations, and communications. I also received a lot of training through the management company located in Fargo. I frequently made presentations to the hospital board regarding the latest expansion plans.

A local attorney, Neil Fleming, was president of the hospital board. He and my friend Jack were frequently at odds over how to run the hospital and nursing home, and since Neil knew that Jack and I were friends, he would try to discount any of the new projects I presented to the board (primarily to cement his sense of power with the group). In my experience, Neil was a bully.

Between 1985-1986, one of the new projects under consideration was a congregate living facility to be built near the nursing home on the west edge of town. The hospital board had received a gift of a one-million-dollar trust from a wealthy farmer. Interest rates were high in the 1980s, and some of the board members wanted to simply invest the funds in stocks. Others wanted to pay cash for the senior apartment complex and avoid debt. There was a lot of in-fighting over this project.

In addition, the concept of congregate living for seniors was new. Most people in the community didn't understand the idea of an apartment building with shared social spaces and adaptations like wide doorways and handrails for support, where seniors could "age in place." Dr. Larson was against the project, and very vocal about his views. Left unsaid was the fact that the clinic wouldn't receive any direct benefit from the project.

Neil Fleming was a lawyer in Cavalier, where his family had homesteaded in the early 1900s. He was a Vietnam veteran (1968-1970) and became a member of the Catholic Church through marriage, although he was raised a Presbyterian. The locals who were familiar with the Fleming family often mused, "There must be a God. Neil and Charlotte (his wife) found each other" (meaning neither blended well into the fabric of the community). Charlotte and Neil met at UND. She wasn't from Cavalier or Pembina County. During the time I lived in Cavalier, they had four children.

Even though his family had deep roots in the area, Neil was not well liked. His social activities were generally relegated to the groups he controlled. Charlotte focused on raising her family and didn't have a lot of friends outside of the local Catholic Church. I never knew who their friends were. Neil and Charlotte Fleming were never included in Jack's social events. I often acted as the hostess at social events at his home, so I knew that there were certain people that Jack wouldn't invite to his home. Neil was one of them. Neil had two brothers, one who was a local farmer and another who had a career in state politics. Their father, Charlie, was also active in local politics, and had served as president of the local hospital board from 1945, when it was in the planning stages, until 1976.

He was also president of the county fair association from 1931-1952.[4]

Charlie died just months before I moved to Cavalier. As the oldest son, Neil *inherited* the family business—running the local hospital and the Pembina County Fair. Neil also added the Cavalier Catholic Church and the Legion Club to the organizations he controlled. If he didn't get his way in community groups, he would pull the "lawyer card" and insinuate that he knew more than everyone else, which basically kept anyone from challenging him.

There was often a power struggle between the physicians and the hospital administration. Neil would often use his position as hospital board president to threaten all of the board members, especially Jack, who represented the physicians. Jack supported the proposed senior apartment project, but Neil didn't. During this debate regarding the apartment building project, I planned a hospital board retreat in Winnipeg, at which it was obvious that no one in the group liked socializing with Neil. He sat alone at dinner!

I remember after a hospital event that I planned and hosted for a retiring hospital administrator when Neil suddenly showed up for the after-party at Jack's house—uninvited. Neil had tagged along with the group from the hospital's management company. (The managers were invited, but Neil was not.)

Jack asked me how Neil got into his house. I told him that he simply followed the guests from the management company, even though he wasn't included in the invitation. Jack was furious, which was rare for him, since he was such an easy-going kind of guy.

AIDS

I was working at the Cavalier hospital in 1982 when HIV (Human Immunodeficiency Virus) was discovered. HIV is the virus responsible for AIDS or Acquired Immuno-Deficiency Syndrome. The US Centers for Disease Control (CDC) published an article about the disease in June 1981, marking the start of awareness of the AIDS epidemic in the United States. At that time, there were four known ways to contract the virus: (1) blood transfusion; (2) homosexual activity; (3) heroin and shared-needle use; or (4) contacts originating in Haiti. The new hospital administrator had a lab background and quickly realized the implications. The lab staff began to wear gowns, masks, and gloves all day.

In September 1983, I had just returned to work following maternity leave. One of my assignments was to send a letter notifying everyone who had surgery at the hospital during the time the blood supply was potentially compromised with HIV-infected blood. The letter said that the 323 patients who fell into this category could have a free blood test to see if they had been infected. I remember that only fourteen individuals responded.

Because I had had a C-section during this time period, I rushed down to the Medical Records Department and asked to see my chart. Fortunately, my surgery hadn't required a transfusion. I never heard that anyone locally had AIDS while I lived in Cavalier.

AIDS didn't seem to make much of an impact in Cavalier, initially, and I don't recall ever thinking particularly about Jack and AIDS, until shortly before

Christmas 1985. Jack returned from a vacation with a stack of presents, and the first thing he said to me was, "I got a clean bill of health." Suddenly I realized why he'd been depressed lately and couldn't sleep: he thought he was sick. Today, I regret that I didn't listen better or recognize that he was presenting an opening to talk about it.

Also in 1985, the famous movie star Rock Hudson died of AIDS at age fifty-nine, and the world learned that he was gay. This became the impetus to make the entire country aware of the AIDS epidemic. Several other famous people were diagnosed with AIDS over the next few years.

In 1986, the National AIDS Education Program was launched to raise awareness across this country. At this point in time, AIDS was not fully understood, and there were no known cures. People were wary because there wasn't a lot of research and very few facts about how AIDS was contracted. People were afraid of this new disease, and they didn't know how to react to their homosexual friends and family. For example, was it okay to shake hands with them?

Looking back, it reminds me of the COVID-19 pandemic in 2020, when no one knew what the implications of the new disease meant. In the mid-1980s, AIDS was a new disease and very little was known about autoimmune deficiency, so the World Health Organization (WHO) launched World AIDS Awareness Day on December 1, 1988,[5] to help people understand this disease and its impact.

When Jack started discussing his health with me, I did wonder if he had HIV/AIDS. His ex-wife told everyone that he was gay before she left town in 1980, although I never saw or heard anything that would support her claim. As a result of his autopsy in February 1986, Jack was diagnosed with kidney cancer, so he certainly was correct—there was something wrong with his health.

7. Changes in Our Lives

Pregnant

EVENTUALLY, MY OFFICE WAS MOVED from the nursing home to the hospital, in a small workspace located across the hall from the administrator's office and a short distance from the doctors' lounge. Since Jack and I both worked at the hospital, he would often stop in my office to visit and share the latest family or community gossip. He also liked to "pull rank" and get me out of hospital meetings to discuss upcoming social events.

I had an ashtray for Jack on the desk in my office, although no one else smoked there. There were no rules about the doctors smoking, and Jack often had a cigarette while he was making rounds, so no one questioned him smoking in my office.

Three years after I married Mike, I thought I might be pregnant. In 1982, you wouldn't want to buy an early pregnancy test in Cavalier if you wanted any privacy. Jack told me to pee in a cup and leave it in his car in the clinic parking lot. He promised to have it analyzed in the clinic lab so that no one would know whose sample it was. The plan was for him to call me at work and simply say "yes" or "no" and hang up, which he did.

Consequently, my friend Jack knew I was pregnant before my husband did.

In 1983, ultrasounds were still primitive. The test did not reveal the gender of the baby, but we had chosen the names Jack Oliver and Sarah Sadie (after Grandma Sadie). I often told friends that I named Baby Jack after my good friend, Jack, who was known as "Uncle" Jack after he was born.

Jack was not my physician for the pregnancy, but he was my friend and my support system. During the pregnancy, I often called him at home to ask questions. In the fall of 1982, I even complained to Jack that it was difficult to find maternity clothes that fit my style, and I wasn't sure what I would wear for the holidays. Jack volunteered to shop for me while he was in New York City on vacation. I gave him my credit card, and when he returned, he had several dresses for me.

Me, pregnant in one of the dresses Jack bought for me.

I asked him how he was able to find the right size, and he told me that he simply found someone in the store who was about my size and had them try on his choices. Later, I wore one of the dresses for New Year's Eve 1982, and another for Grandma Sadie's funeral in February 1983. I loved those clothes and kept them for many years!

Baby Jack Arrives

The morning of Sunday, May 8, 1983, I awoke to water running down my leg. I immediately called Jack at home, who said, "Your water broke. You're going to have the baby today! I'll call the hospital, get everything ready, and call you back." I already knew, since I had been diagnosed with placenta previa that I would be having a cesarean section. Surgery was scheduled for 3:00 p.m., to accommodate Dr. Tareen, the local surgeon, who had previously scheduled a racket ball session at the Cavalier Air Force Station.

"Baby Jack" was born on Mother's Day afternoon, the first grandchild on either side of our family. I stayed in the hospital for almost one week. This length of stay was standard procedure following a C-section at that time. (Today, the Cavalier hospital no longer delivers babies at all.) Grandpa Oliver was excited to know that the family name would carry on and promptly established a college fund in his grandson's name.

Jack Wahl planned a celebration event for my parents and Mike's dad. The party was held at Jack's house, and he planned every detail. I think he was as excited about the baby as anyone in either my family or Mike's.

Fourteen babies were born that week in May 1983, so it was unusually busy in the small hospital where there were only six bassinets available for newborns. Many of those babies later became life-long friends with my son, Jack. Most of the babies were delivered by our friend Jack, a primary care physician. "Uncle" Jack would always stop by my room whenever he was at the hospital delivering someone's baby. It didn't matter what time of day or night it was! He liked to flip on the light and say, "You're not pregnant anymore. Let's have a smoke!"

Jack would tease me after Baby Jack was born, since he was an attending physician in my delivery. Joking, he'd say, "How many of your friends have seen your liver?"

I would always ask him, "Does it look like I drink too much?"

And he would reply, "Do you really want to know?"

Reality hit. I was a mom, wholly responsible for my newborn's well-being. Even though I had often cared for three younger brothers, when the time came for cutting fingernails and temperature-taking, I called Jack, who came and gave me instructions and a demonstration. Everyone should have a friend like Jack.

Baby Jack was eight months old when Grandpa Oliver remarried in 1983 and moved to Grand Forks to live with Marge and her children. Oliver was her third husband (though she was just a couple of years older than my husband, Mike). Oliver liked to say that at least Marge didn't marry him for his money, because she had more than he did! We liked to remind him that she had financial resources due to her two previous marriages to wealthy men. She went on to marry a fourth wealthy man from Grand Forks after she and Oliver divorced, so I guess she proved our point!

Oliver retired and turned over the business to Mike and Mark. Mark was still living rent-free in his dad's house, which Oliver wanted to keep as a respite, a place to get away. Sometimes he needed a break from Marge and her children. After marrying Marge, Oliver was basically estranged from his Cavalier friends, although he still owned the home next door to Jack Wahl. Marge and Jack never appreciated each other.

Annette

I was still in the hospital after Baby Jack was born, and Annette, one of the hospital housekeepers, was cleaning my room. She told me that she had come to the US from Scotland as a nanny twenty-five years earlier. She had lived in London, Ontario, and cared for three children of a couple who were both professors. When the children grew up, they no longer needed a nanny, and she was let go.

Eventually, Annette moved to Winnipeg and met a widower from Pembina County. She married him while in her late thirties but was now a widow with a son who was going to graduate from high school that spring. Her son, John, had joined the military and would be leaving the area.

While she was sweeping the floor in my hospital room, Annette said, "Let me know if you ever need a babysitter. I have no family and John will soon be gone. Other than this job, I have nothing to do."

I quickly realized that the hospital housekeepers are the only employees who can do their jobs and visit with the patients too. I later utilized this knowledge in the hospitals where I worked in marketing and communications. I got some great ideas from the housekeepers over the years!

It didn't take long for me to call Annette and ask her to babysit Jack. She became a member of our family immediately. My parents lived two hundred miles away, and since both of them were still working, they weren't available to help. Oliver had moved to Grand Forks and probably wouldn't have been interested in helping anyway, and Mike's mother was no longer alive.

Baby Jack was just a couple of months old, and I was still on maternity leave when I asked my husband to stay home with the baby while I went to the grocery store. On my way home with the groceries, I met Mike driving back to the car dealership. Where was the baby? I was frantic!

Later, I questioned Mike about leaving the baby to return to work. His response was, "Well, he was sleeping, so I thought it wouldn't matter." From that day on, I never left home without a babysitter on site, even when Mike was at home. And I often took the baby with me if I had to go out of town.

Annette frequently stayed with Baby Jack when Mike and I would leave town together. I was totally comfortable leaving her with the baby because she was so dedicated. Annette was more of a *real* grandparent than any of his living grandparents.[6] I am forever grateful for her support and love of my kids.

Annette, our nanny, with Jack and Sarah.

The Challenger Explodes

Through a 1986 Ford Motor Company sales contest at the family car dealership, Mike won a trip to Super Bowl XX in New Orleans. Baby Jack was almost three years old and stayed home with Annette. We flew to New Orleans and saw the Chicago Bears and New England Patriots play at the famous Superdome on January 26, 1986. Chicago won the Vince Lombardi trophy, 46-10.

After the Super Bowl, we flew to Cancún, Mexico, for the second part of our trip. While we were in the air

Mike, me, and friends at the Super Bowl.

and flying over the Gulf of Mexico, the US Space Shuttle Challenger exploded near Florida. We learned of the disastrous January 28, 1986, space accident when we arrived at our hotel.

About the same time, Jack Wahl had flown to Phoenix for a Super Bowl party at Jack and Bev Mayo's winter home. The Mayo's owned a construction company and lived in Cavalier during good weather. We were all back in Cavalier in early February, and we got together to exchange stories of our travels and the shock of the Challenger explosion.

There are some events that happen during a lifetime that remind you of where you were when a life-changing event happened. For example, most people, if they are old enough, remember where they were when President Kennedy was assassinated. I associate the explosion of the Challenger with my friend Jack's death. I was thirty-four years old at the time. Today I'm sixty-eight, so for over half of my life I've been making that connection.

8. The Murder

Late Nights

CAVALIER DIDN'T HAVE A TWENTY-FOUR-HOUR restaurant, and the bars closed at 1:00 a.m. It was common for Jack Wahl to invite people to his home to continue partying when the local bars closed. Some were strangers Jack had just met, but most of the local, late-night visitors were single men who had nowhere else to go and few responsibilities. In February, many of them didn't have much work to do on the family farm or their local businesses either, so there was no reason to rush home.

One reason that Jack invited people to his home frequently was that he was lonely. I know this because we often talked about it. I was a friend and confidant. He talked to me about personal things, and I assumed that since he had a lot of friends, he talked with them in the same way. I didn't realize until after he was gone that I was part of his inner circle.

Jack had been in Stu's Pub on Wednesday, February 12, 1986, the night of his murder. Stu's Pub was previously known as "Dick's Bar," although the entire time I lived in Cavalier, the "D" had fallen off and it simply said "ick's Bar," until it was sold to Stuart Askew and renamed "Stu's Pub." The bar was also famous for a lump in the floor near the front entrance, which I know I tripped over every time I ever went there.

Wine was my drink of choice, but neither Stu's Pub nor Dick's Bar stocked wine glasses, although they had wine in a box. When I had wine there, it was usually served in a highball glass. The bartender would serve the wine with ice unless you told him or her not to add the "rocks."

Stu's Pub was located on the main thoroughfare going through town, near the intersection of Division Avenue and Main Street, which today sports the town's only traffic signal. (It was a three-way stop when I lived in Cavalier.) Main Street is actually State Highway 5, which leads to the Renwick Dam and then Langdon, North Dakota, thirty-five miles to the west. Division Avenue is part of State Highway 18. The odd intersection in the center of town follows an old oxen trail the Indians utilized to get to Winnipeg before the area was settled by homesteaders.

Stu's Pub was located approximately halfway between the Cedar Inn Steakhouse and Lounge on the south end of town, and Wahl's neighborhood on the north side of town. Most people would know the owners of the cars parked nearby, and if they spotted a friend's car, they would stop at Stu's on the way home to say hello. They might avoid Stu's Pub if they saw a car belonging to someone they didn't wish to see too.

One time, I was at the Cedar Inn Lounge with friends. We were the only group in the bar when Eileen, the bartender said, "This place is boring. Let's go to Dick's (Stu's Pub)," and we did. I was careful to grab a wine glass prior to leaving.

Another notable incident that happened at Stu's Pub was when a local man stumbled across the street wearing no pants. Most bars and restaurants in North Dakota featured signs that said, "No shirt, no shoes, no service." Since the man was wearing a shirt and shoes, he qualified to be served!

Julie Young, the bartender at Stu's Pub, was very friendly, and although she wasn't a local, she knew everyone in town through her work. She was one of the last people to see Jack alive. Julie was interviewed by Pembina County Deputy Sheriff Joe Martindale and Special Agent David Lybeck of the North Dakota Bureau of Criminal Investigations (BCI) at 8:00 p.m. on February 13. She corroborated the information the officials had gathered from the bar patrons and added that Jack left the bar around closing time and that he was alone. She also stated that Dr. Wahl often invited groups of customers to his house to continue party-ing after the bar closed. She had been invited there once too. It was generally known that a regular group of young and single local men would frequently take up Jack's invitation. They knew that there would be unlimited booze and probably food too, but Julie said there was no invitation from Jack that night.

This group of twenty-something, local single guys moved between jobs and had various run-ins with law enforcement, including driving under the influence (DUI), driving with a suspended license, and some drug arrests. Some had served jail time for misdemeanors. Dean Becker, Matt Hughes, and Charlie Kippen were often in the group that partied at Wahl's after the bars closed, however these three weren't in Stu's Pub the night of February 12. Oddly, Dean Becker was the only one interviewed by the local investigators regarding the murder who *wasn't* at Stu's Pub on February 12.

John Nelson (no relationship to me) was one of the young, single guys who had previously been to parties at Jack's house. He was drinking in Stu's Pub with the bowling crew on February 12. All of the young men who were in Stu's Pub that night were interviewed by the investigators the next day.

The Next Morning

I was at work in my office at the hospital early on the morning of Thursday, February 13, 1986, when I suddenly heard an overhead page alerting the ambulance staff and the physicians to go to the emergency room. Next, I heard several people running down the hallway. This was unusual, and although I was curious, I stayed at my desk.

Part of my job at the hospital was communicating with the media, although there were few opportunities to interact with the local *Cavalier Chronicle* or the regional *Grand Forks Herald*. There had only been two large, media-worthy stories since I started working at the hospital.

The first emergency took place during Labor Day weekend the previous September. A farmer had been burning his fields near Interstate 29. The fire spread, assisted by an untimely windstorm, resulting in an eighteen-car pileup on I-29. Our little hospital was the closest crisis center. The tiny emergency room quickly filled up with injured patients, many of whom were Canadians heading north to Manitoba after the long weekend.

The other incident occurred at Christmastime, when a mentally ill patient escaped from a secured room on the second floor of the hospital. He proceeded to hold two nurses and one of the doctors as hostages. The patient wielded a knife, and the incident went on for several hours.

When I heard people running in the hospital hallway, I knew that something big was underway. Later I learned that in addition to two members of the ambulance crew, the four remaining physicians had rushed over to Jack's house when the emergency call came in from Jack's housekeeper.

The Housekeeper

Dr. Wahl's housekeeper, Betty Hanson, arrived at his house for a weekly cleaning on Thursday morning, February 13, 1986, as planned. She had a key to the house, but it wasn't needed. The front door was not only unlocked but wide open. When she removed her shoes, she noted that the floor was very cold, so the door had to have been open for quite a while. The door to the greenhouse at the front of the house was closed, which was atypical too.

Betty Hanson was a hard worker who had a variety of small jobs to augment her social security income. She wasn't highly educated and had never made a lot of money. Now, as a widow in her sixties, she was totally responsible for herself. At least her kids were grown and on their own.

Betty had cleaned Jack's house previously when he lived in the development on the west side of town, so she had worked for him for several years. Jack's new house was more than twice the size of his original home. He paid her more for cleaning when he moved to his new, large home. Betty was just happy to have a job, and Jack wasn't very demanding.

I was a frequent visitor at Jack's house, and it was not spotless, even with a housekeeper. Drink glasses would sit around for days following a social gathering, just waiting for Betty's arrival, when she would tidy up the rooms. Betty was really good at cleaning the carpet. You could see the lines the vacuum made during any visit to the house, whether it was the day after she cleaned or six days later. I always admired her skill.

The first thing Betty usually did when she arrived for the weekly cleaning was to check Jack's garage to see if he had left for work, but she didn't do this on that cold February morning because, upon arriving at 8:35 a.m., she heard a noise from the basement. The door to the basement entrance was open, which was unusual, so she went to the basement staircase to see what was going on, wiping her hands on the handrail as she usually did to check for dust as she descended to the lower level.

Betty was used to being in the large house alone, so she was surprised to hear noise. Jack hadn't mentioned having visitors. She soon discovered the voices were coming from the projection television system downstairs in the family room, and she went to retrieve the remote control to turn it off. That's when she saw a body face-down on the floor, near the sectional couch. At first, she thought someone was sleeping there. The body appeared to be covered loosely by a winter overcoat, like a blanket. Timidly, she lifted the coat and realized it was Jack, and he was covered in blood. She noted that there appeared to be blood all over the couch too.

No doubt shocked, Betty lit a cigarette, took a drag and then quickly put it out in an empty beer can on the cabinet located on the north wall. She knew that she had to call but she wasn't sure if she should call the ambulance or the hospital or the police. There wasn't a 9-1-1 system at that time. She decided to call the hospital and ran upstairs.

The Emergency Team Arrives

The ambulance staff and the clinic occupied the same block with the hospital campus, so both the doctors and the ambulance crew were in close proximity to the health care facilities. The Pembina County Sheriff's office would also have had access to the ambulance call through the shared emergency telecommunications system.

Betty waited outside after making the call. It was February, so she was glad that she had grabbed her coat. Betty met the emergency crew outside and told them to go downstairs. She was sobbing by the time they arrived, and since she didn't know what she was supposed to do, she simply waited outside in the cold air and lit another cigarette.

In her interview with the investigators later that first day, she explained that she used the stairwell, so fingerprints may have been ruined. She also confessed that she put a cigarette out in one of the empty beer cans. Betty was worried that she might have compromised the investigation.

The Investigation Begins

Dr. Jensen arrived with two EMTs, and they hurried into the house through the front door which was unlocked. The door lock was also broken, so it didn't close tightly. Dr. Tareen, who lived next door, later stated that he had been called to the hospital in the middle of the previous night and had noticed that Jack's front door was ajar. He didn't stop to check on him, though. (He regrets that decision today.)

Dr. Jensen found Jack on the floor near the sectional couch, loosely covered by a winter overcoat. He also wore his sweater jacket, which was pulled up over his arms. Dr. Jensen quickly opened his shirt and felt for a heartbeat. The television was still on, and it was so loud that the doctor asked one of the EMTs to turn it off, so he could listen for vital signs. There were no signs of life. Dr. Jensen estimated the time of death as around 2:00 a.m. He called the Pembina County Sheriff's phone number and asked for assistance at Wahl's house. Pembina County Deputy Sheriff Joe Martindale arrived about fifteen minutes later.

Suddenly, the group was startled by the telephone ringing, but when Dr. Jensen answered the call, the caller hung up without saying anything. Soon Drs. Larson, Watkin, and Tareen joined the others in the basement family room. They could see blood and assumed that Jack had been shot. They knew better than to move the body before law enforcement arrived. Only later that afternoon, when the body was lifted from the floor to a gurney, did investigators realize that the wounds were from a stabbing.

Because Pembina County Sheriff Glenn Wells was on vacation, Deputy Sheriff Martindale led the law enforcement group. He had received the call around 8:45 a.m. and headed straight to Wahl's house. My understanding is that the protocol for a murder investigation would put the Pembina County state's attorney in the lead, but in this case the county sheriff's office took charge. I know that all of the law enforcement personnel worked together out of an office attached to the Pembina County courthouse, including the state highway patrol and the Cavalier City police. The hierarchy and reporting systems were blurry in a small town where everyone knew each other and, in the case of law enforcement, worked together too.

By the time Deputy Martindale arrived, seven people had already visited the murder site: Drs. Jensen, Larson, Tareen, and Watkin; two EMTs; and Betty Hanson. Thus, less than nine hours after the murder occurred, this group walked through Jack's house, destroying at least footprint evidence, as they headed to the basement level. I remember that later when

Sonny Dump, the BCI officer got involved, he asked all of the doctors to turn in their shoes as part of the investigation.

I don't know if the law enforcement officers wore gloves, because it wasn't required by OSHA (Title 29) until 1991, but the medical personnel were diligent and wore them, because they were cognizant of blood-borne pathogens.

I would guess that the individuals who had never been in Jack's house were almost as interested in his house as in the body, since the group consisted of more medical and emergency support than law enforcement. Did they park in the driveway or on the street? I'm quite sure they weren't thinking about collecting evidence as they arrived.

Deputy Sheriff Martindale eventually told the medical personnel to leave. The law enforcement part of the investigation had begun, so the doctors returned to the hospital and huddled in the doctors' lounge.

Martindale next asked John Reynolds, the Cavalier police chief, who had just arrived, to secure the house. He then placed a call to the office of North Dakota Bureau of Criminal Investigations (BCI) and asked for Sonny Dump, who was stationed in Grafton, to come to Cavalier for a homicide investigation. Officer Dump arrived around 1:00 p.m.

Two additional Pembina County deputies, agents Alan Latozke and Wayne Samdahl, were also summoned to Wahl's house by Martindale. By the time Sonny Dump arrived, Pembina County District Attorney Bob Lee had also made his way to Wahl's house, along with BCI Special Agent David Lybeck, and Mel Stark, manager of the Cavalier Clinic. This is a typical small-town reaction to a big event. Everyone who thinks he has a role wants to be part of the initial discussion.

The Crime Scene and Evidence

Jack was found lying on the floor in front of the couch with his sweater jacket pulled up over his head, his arms still in the sleeves. Blood covered the couch. A coat was casually thrown over the body. Both Joe and Sonny had cameras. They took photos and videotaped the crime scene. (I would assume that they looked for fingerprints and studied any blood splatter, but since the murder occurred prior to DNA technology, they wouldn't have saved evidence as they would today.)

The investigators noted that there were two cans of Miller Lite beer, and another can of Coors beer on the coffee table, along with an ashtray full of cigarette butts. These items were taken as evidence and secured in evidence containers. Next, the immediate crime scene was taped off so no evidence would be compromised. Evidence tape was added to the doors and windows, an alarm was installed, and additional locks were placed on the doors.

When BCI Agent David Lybeck arrived, he observed that the murder scene didn't indicate a struggle of any kind. According to the investigation notes, both Lybeck and Sonny Dump noted a wound to the back of Jack's body and some side wounds. BCI Agent Sonny Dump added that it looked like the murderer was left-handed, from the angle of the wounds, or that the stabbing took place from behind the couch where Jack had fallen asleep.

Referring to the empty beer cans, Agent Sonny Dump noted that there were no Lite beers in the downstairs refrigerator located behind the bar. Dr. Tareen added that Jack didn't like Lite beer. The ashtray on the table was filled with Now cigarette butts, the brand Jack smoked.

BCI Agent Sonny Dump also reported in his investigation notes, "The victim was lying on his left side with his right foot and leg raised. His left leg was under the coffee table, and the victim's head was against the couch. The couch had bloody handprints, and there appeared to be blood splatter on the couch. The victim was fully clothed, and his light tan jacket was pulled up over his head. There were no signs of a struggle." (I believe that Jack had fallen asleep or was passed out from drinking when he was attacked.)

I learned more about the status of the artifacts taken from the crime scene when I met with Deputy Sheriff Marcus Ramsay in July 2021, in Cavalier. He told me that the remaining samples from the murder scene were not stored safely and that the exhibits had deteriorated. He doubted whether the remaining items could help a new investigation, even with today's technology. In addition, the courthouse where the evidence was stored had been remodeled in 1994, and some items had been discarded. Since both Sheriff Glenn Wells and Deputy Sheriff Martindale had died, as well as Sonny Dump, the Bureau of Criminal Investigations detective, there was no one to discuss the evidence that had been gathered from the crime scene.

As part of the investigation, Pembina County Deputy Sheriff Martindale and BCI Agent Sonny Dump documented that they had secured homosexual pornography, both magazines and books, from Jack's bedroom. They also walked through the house with the housekeeper, Betty Hanson, and asked her if anything seemed out of place. Betty told the officers that she never saw any homosexual materials in Jack's house and that everything seemed normal—nothing was out of place, but that she was aware of the broken door to his bedroom. She estimated that it had happened in October, and said that Jack was in the process of having it repaired.

9. Personal Aftermath

D R. JENSEN BROKE THE NEWS to me when he returned to the hospital. He was very open with me about what he knew from the investigation. Later, he accompanied me from the hospital to the family car dealership to tell my husband that our friend Jack was dead. After telling him what we knew, my husband took me home. I was in shock. How could this happen?

Mike decided that we should call his dad, now living with Marge in Grand Forks, and let him know the sad news. Oliver answered the phone (no one had cell phones, yet) and Marge, his wife, picked up the call on another extension. Mike explained what we knew and asked his dad to come to Cavalier.

Marge spoke up immediately and said that Oliver couldn't go to Cavalier because her son had a concert that night, and they would be going to the event. Marge still had her four teenagers living with her.

Later in the day, Dr. Warren Jensen called to tell me that they had moved the body to the local funeral home and discovered that Jack had been stabbed six times. They were sending the body for autopsy to Grand Forks, North Dakota.

Grand Forks Herald

ar, Issue 234 · Copyright 1986 Grand Forks Herald.   Grand Forks, N.D., Friday, February 14, 1986   Four Sections. 32 Pages   ★★   Price 15¢
Law By Carrier

Cavalier doctor stabbed; authorities call it murder

By Ann Bailey
and Mike Brue
Herald Staff Writers

CAVALIER, N.D. — John D. Wahl, a popular Cavalier doctor, was found dead in his home Thursday morning with multiple stab wounds in his body. Authorities said the death was being investigated as a murder.

No arrests had been made by Thursday evening. Pembina County State's Attorney Robert Lee said authorities could offer no motive for the suspected murder, which they speculated recurred about 2 a.m. Thursday.

Investigators said they found no weapon. They refused to comment about any signs of a struggle.

Pembina County Chief Deputy Joe Martindale said nothing appeared to be missing from Wahl's house. He said Wahl was known to keep $2n$ tiques and other valuable items there.

Wahl was known to his friends as

Photography: Ken Kle

*The day after the murder, Grand Forks Herald, page one
(photo credit: Ken Kleven).*

Stabbing was the worst thing we could have imagined. When someone is shot with a gun, the perpetrator is at a distance. In a stabbing, there is no physical distance. The thought of someone touching Jack while killing him was just too hard to take! I went to bed and refused to talk to anyone.

Questions, Speculation, and Rumor

Many times, I've wished that I had been with Jack that night; perhaps it would have altered the course of events. But the last night my friend Jack was alive and enjoying his dinner at the Cedar Inn Steakhouse and Lounge, I was at a neighbor's home, drinking some Mogen David wine they had received as a Christmas gift. We joked that we were having communion, unaware that everything was about to change.

It's difficult to accept a murder anytime, but when it remains unsolved for so many years, it makes you question everyone around you, especially in a small town. Jack was *just* a friend. I can't image how I would feel if my spouse, a sibling, or my child had been murdered, and the case had gone cold—though many others endure this experience.

I was devastated. First, I had lost the one friend in Cavalier who kept me sane. And second, there didn't seem to be any answers as to *who* would want to kill Jack or *why* he was killed. Local law enforcement didn't release regular updates, so the community grapevine was ripe with gossip and theories.

Eventually, our Cavalier friends "chose sides," and I no longer wanted to socialize with those who believed that Jack was gay and that his lifestyle was the key to the murder. I was lucky to have friends from college and from my hometown and Grand Forks and Fargo, to at least talk to on the telephone. But a chasm had opened in my life, and socially, nothing was the same.

Mike and I left town more often and spent more time with our old friends from college. We also didn't know what to think about the rumors of Jack's other life. The police and the media seemed to expose Jack's secrets, but we had never seen anything to indicate that Jack was gay. We didn't know what to believe!

The Gay Theory

One theory about the murder emerged quickly and never really was dispelled: essentially, that Jack's gay lifestyle was at the root of the crime. I rejected this on several fronts, first and foremost because it blamed the victim.

If the Kinsey Report, published in 1948, is to be accepted, one out of ten people have homosexual tendencies. That means there were approximately one hundred fifty gay men and women living in the small town of Cavalier in 1986.

I don't know of many straight men who have gay friends, but several of our friends were openly gay, and we often socialized with them. I don't know what this says, and I'm not implying anything. I'm simply including it in this story because I believe it is unusual. For example, during college, Mark Gregory lived with one of our friends who "came out of the closet" after graduation, surprising most of us who knew Bill, as well as the other roommates. Our friend Bill died of AIDS in 1989.

After the murder, Mark was one of the first young, single men interviewed by local law enforcement. The police seemed to be exploring the "gay angle" above all others. During his interview, Deputy Sheriff Joe Martindale spoke up on Mark's behalf, stating, "I caught him fucking a girl during high school out in the sand hills. He's not gay!" This comment by an authority figure saved Mark from further questioning. The investigation notes indicate that Mark stated that he had a girlfriend. When asked if Jack Wahl ever approached him in a sexual way, Mark responded, "No, never."

Mark Gregory would simply have no reason to be angry with Jack. They were neighbors and friends. Jack had recently helped Mark with his new medical diagnosis, and Jack knew all the Gregory family's medical histories. They both liked to party a lot and were simply two of the many single men living in Cavalier with not much to do after work. Jack was like another family member. There would simply be no motivation for Mark to kill Jack.

If I had had an opportunity to speak to law enforcement representatives, I would have pointed out that I had spilled white wine in the living room near the fireplace on the previous Thursday, when I was there with Dr. Maxine Rasmussen. I have always wondered if they looked at that spot as evidence from the night of the murder.

Another thing that has always bothered me regarding the investigation is that I knew that the outside doorknobs to Jack's house had all been broken in the fall of 1985—before Halloween. Jack and I had discussed the broken door handles, along with a damaged door to his bedroom, but since Jack was killed in February, if I knew about the broken doors, they didn't happen the night of the murder. Anyway, Jack's house was totally unlocked that night in February 1986, because the locks were broken. The first time I shared this insight was in July 2021 when I met with the current Pembina County Sheriff and his deputy—Sheriff Meidinger and Deputy Ramsay.

There are several different entrances to the house. The murderer could have entered the house through the garage, through Jack's sliding-glass bedroom doors to the deck, or downstairs through two different entrances. I assume that the physicians, deputies, and others all entered Jack's house through the front door, since Betty Hanson was waiting for them there.

For the past thirty-five years, the most prominent unanswered question has been "Was the murder a crime of passion?" In other words, was it related to Jack's sexuality? Newspaper reports along with the investigators' comments have implied that Jack had a questionable social life that put his life in jeopardy. I have always believed that this theory put the blame on Jack himself, and that's just not fair! He was a victim!

That others in Cavalier would embrace this theory was probably inevitable; after all, the media were quoting law enforcement—it must be true! Friends gathered informally at our house the day after the murder. By then, there were several rumors about what could have happened, including a psychotic patient stalking Jack or a wild party that got out of hand. Over the next few days, however, our social group, fueled by wine and other liquor, and stoked by newspaper accounts, quickly formed positions on the murder case. There were Cavalier friends that I never spoke to after that week in February 1986. (This attitude reflected the group of locals who either bought his ex-wife's story that he was gay, or thought he partied too much.)

The Autopsy

Jack's body was initially sent to the local funeral home, and then transferred to the lab at UND for autopsy on Valentine's Day. Three different professionals are involved in investigating an unattended death (defined as when someone dies alone): a coroner, a pathologist, and the medical examiner. Each one has a different perspective and role in the investigation.

Each county in North Dakota has a person assigned to the position of coroner. Jack was the Pembina County coroner at the time of his own death, but the coroner isn't always a physician. In many rural areas, the county coroner is often the local sheriff or a funeral director. In some counties in the US, the coroner is an elected position. In this investigation, Dr. Warren Jensen served as coroner: after reviewing the signs of death, he declared the victim dead.

Pathologists are experts in diagnosing and characterizing diseases. A medical examiner is a physician who determines both the *means* and the *cause* of death. In the case of a homicide, the means may include stabbing, shooting, or strangulation. The cause may be lack of oxygen or bleeding. The medical examiner is involved during the autopsy stage of an investigation.

Following an autopsy, a certificate of death is issued by the state medical examiner. There are four types of cause in an unattended death: accident (35.7 percent), homicide (4.7 percent), suicide (35.7 percent), or natural (18.0 percent) death. Infrequently, and after extensive research, the cause may also be decided as *unknown or undetermined* (5.9 percent).[7]

There are only two locations in North Dakota for autopsies. Approximately half of the annual autopsies are conducted at the UND Medical School. Jack's autopsy was conducted at UND, since Grand Forks was the closest lab. The other North Dakota location is in Bismarck, North Dakota, at the State Crime Lab. It is interesting to note that there are no national, mandatory laboratory standards for autopsies in the US.

Dr. Warren Jensen was the acting county coroner and signed off on the autopsy report, which revealed that Jack had a blood alcohol content of 0.10, and that he had cirrhosis of the liver, an enlarged spleen, mild hardening of the arteries around his heart, and a tumor on his left kidney. It also indicated that there were stab wounds to the liver, lungs, and pulmonary vein, plus two ribs had been fractured. "The victim was stabbed six times, once in the right upper chest, twice on the right side, and three times in the back with a knife-like object." Jack was forty-three years old. The cause of death was homicide, one of ten murders in North Dakota in 1986. He died around 2:00 a.m., Thursday morning, February 13, 1986.

When the autopsy was completed, Dr. Jensen told me about the cancer diagnosis, and I told him what Jack had said about his recent physical. The members of the physician's group were incredulous that Jack hadn't said anything to them about his health and that he had instead shared his health concerns with me. (They weren't aware that he was often depressed and couldn't sleep, either.) The doctors all agreed that Jack Wahl was the best physician in the group to determine a diagnosis and were surprised that he had a health concern.

Two Funerals

There were two funeral services for Jack, one in Cavalier on February 16, 1986, and another at his small hometown church the next day. His casket was closed. The remaining four Cavalier Clinic physicians were pallbearers. Both events were a media circus. There was a law enforcement presence as well.

I remember walking into the funeral home for the Cavalier memorial. It was held on a Sunday at 2:00 p.m. Jack's family, whom I'd met previously, were all in a receiving line. When I introduced myself, one of his sisters said, "You're Baby Jack's Mom. He talked about you all of the time." I was surprised that Jack's family knew about my son. I remember that I was sobbing through the event and couldn't say much to anyone.

Dr. Warren Jensen and I had written a eulogy. We stayed up late, two nights in a row, to complete the project. We couldn't sleep anyway. Dr. Jensen delivered the following at Jack's funeral:

> As friends, we would like to extend our sorrow and deepest sympathy to the family of our dear friend, Jack.
>
> Jack came to Cavalier to begin his practice when we were in need of a physician. He has been serving our needs ever since. To Jack, his profession was more than a job, and his compassion for people made him a refuge for the sick, elderly, and lonely. To his patients, friendship came easily as they felt his genuine concern.
>
> His enthusiasm for his medical practice was inspiring; however, his interests were many. He was especially interested in art and gardening, for beauty was something he loved to share. His life centered on giving.
>
> He will always be remembered for his ability to listen, his wit in conversation, and occasionally his irrepressible opinion. We cannot begin to mention his many acts of kindness during his stay with us. He will always be remembered, for he has touched us all.

His sixteen years with us now seem brief, for we self-ishly yearn for more of his company. I'm proud to say that he was my friend, and we will miss our dear friend very much. Although difficult, we should not look to this day with sadness, for Jack would not wish that.

We should use his example of his compassion for people, appreciation for beauty, and enthusiasm for life, which he has shared with us. This is how we will remember him.

Jack was buried in the St. Olaf Lutheran Church cemetery near his hometown of Hannaford, North Dakota. It's a lonely, rural place in the eastern half of North Dakota. His parents eventually joined him there. Dorothy died in 2001 and Russell in 2010. They were 69 and 71 when their oldest son was murdered in 1986.

Jack's mother was my current age when her son was murdered. She lived for another fifteen years without knowing who killed her oldest son or why. My friend Jack was forty-three when he died. I also have a son named Jack, who is almost that same age now. I can't imagine how Dorothy managed to live with the unsolved murder, never knowing what happened to her son. It certainly haunts me: not knowing who killed a loved one, and of course, why?

One month after the funerals, I learned that I was pregnant. It was a planned pregnancy; we always wanted a second child. I immediately thought it would be another boy, since there were four boys in the Gregory family, I had three brothers, and I had my son, Jack, who would be three in May. I had spent my life to date hanging out with "the guys" more or less, so I had chosen another boy's name for the baby.

I knew that I would have another C-section. There wasn't a NICU, a pediatrician, an OB/GYN, or an anesthetist working at the hospital in Cavalier. Thus, if a mother had one C-section, she would only be allowed to deliver a second child via surgery. There wasn't much of a safety net in the small, fifty-two-bed hospital. The nearest tertiary (full service) hospital was located in Grand Forks, eighty-five miles away.

My family practice doctor, Dr. Larson, was nearing retirement age but still practicing. He figured the due date as October 13, but wouldn't schedule the surgery for the thirteenth, due to his superstitions. "You don't want the baby to have a Friday the 13th birthday some day!" he stated, and scheduled the delivery for Tuesday, October 14. So I had been pregnant for a month before the murder, but didn't know it, yet. My baby was delivered almost exactly eight months after the murder.

Dr. Larson had also delivered my husband's two younger brothers in the 1960s. One of those brothers had died when he was seven, of a congenital heart defect. Mike's youngest brother was mentally challenged. So, in addition to being depressed, I worried about the heredity factors and also fetal alcohol syndrome, because I had been drinking a lot. Dr. Larson reviewed Susan Gregory's chart to see if there were any indications of heredity factors, but charting was so primitive in the 1960s, when John and James were born, that he didn't learn much.

Only those who have lived in a small town can appreciate what it is like to have a doctor deliver your baby, when the previous week you saw him in church, or at a school event, or had dinner with him and his spouse.

I remember hearing my doctor describe cutting through someone's fat layers to deliver her baby, and I knew that mother! He told the story in the bar at the Cedar Inn Steakhouse and Lounge, and I wasn't the only one to hear his description. I was eight months pregnant at the time.

Life in a small town is different. There is no anonymity and no privacy. In my case, I had just been through a traumatic experience involving all of the local doctors within the past year. I spoke with them frequently since I worked at the hospital. We often shared new information about the murder investigation. Now, here we were just eight months past the night of the murder, planning my C-section.

When the time came for the delivery, one doctor administered anesthesia, another one made the incision for my C-section, one of them pulled the baby from my body, and another doctor stitched me up. Meanwhile, Uncle Mark, Jim Salaba, and Kenny Askew were in the waiting room with Mike. Like I've stated previously, I spent most of my life with "the guys." Annette was at home with our son Jack.

We didn't know the baby's gender in advance. Eventually, I remember being rolled out of the operating room and hearing Dr. Jensen say, "You have a beautiful baby girl, what's her name?" I responded, "Sarah Sadie." She was perfect and still is, thirty-five years later. Thank you, God!

10. Notes from the Investigation

The Murder Weapon

LOCAL LAW ENFORCEMENT OFFICERS SURMISED that whoever killed Jack was familiar with where the vital organs were located in a body. The investigators speculated that perhaps the murderer was another physician or a veteran. (It was obviously someone who was trained to kill or knew human anatomy.) Jack was stabbed six times. The murder weapon was never found, and the only reference to the size of the blade in the investigation documents was that it was one-inch wide, according to the notes submitted by Officer David Lybeck from the North Dakota Bureau of Criminal Investigations on February 16, 1986.[8]

The Case Theory

One of the things I have learned about murder investigations is that they usually begin with a working theory. As the investigation evolves, the investigators work to stack the evidence to support their theory (just like O.J. Simpson and the famous glove). Prior to 1986, I thought that investigations were objective and based on the clues that surfaced.

The working theory of law enforcement was that Jack was gay, and since the murder was so violent, it was some type of gay revenge, possibly a relationship gone awry. Apparently, Dr. David Watkin was one of the earliest proponents of this theory—speculating about this in Jack's home while the body still lay in the family room—and the police also quickly latched on to it, especially Pembina County Deputy Alan Latozke.[9] Even though Dr. Watkin was the only one of the doctors who never socialized with Jack, he nevertheless verbalized the following to the investigators: "Over the years, Jack had a lot of late-night visitors. People would come at ungodly hours. Many were strangers. Was there anything missing?" At this point in the investigation notes, BCI Agent Lybeck volunteered, "We've learned that he was definitely a homosexual." There was no basis for this statement recorded in the notes.

Dr. Watkin's comments surprised me when I reviewed the investigator's notes, since he would know the least about Jack's life after work. I can only guess that he was regurgitating the thoughts of those community members who questioned Jack's lifestyle, and that he was anxious to position himself as some kind of authority.

In response to Dr. Watkin's question about missing items, North Dakota BCI Agent Sonny Dump said that several people mentioned that Jack always wore a Concordia College ring. "We haven't found that yet, but we will work with the housekeeper to go through the whole house to see if she notices anything missing." All of the physicians agreed that Jack always wore that Concordia '64 ring.

Dave Watkin added, "If Jack picked someone up after he left Stu's Pub, they wouldn't have had a car . . . there were so many doggone people who would come and go. . . ." Dr. Watkin continued, "If I was going to bump Jack off, it would be for a large amount of money . . . we've been worried . . . Jack would be the best person to go after in this whole world! He was a public figure, but he's got a secret he's tried to keep quiet all of these years. He'd be a perfect person to blackmail . . . you should check his bank accounts and meet with the other homosexuals who live in the area."[10]

Dr. Watkin then added that he had looked in Jack's bedroom when he first arrived at the house, and that the bed was unmade. There was an empty suitcase in the room. The empty suitcase wasn't a surprise to me, since Jack had just returned from a trip to Phoenix and was planning to leave for Las Vegas, Nevada, on February 21, 1986.

Dr. Warren Jensen interrupted, "The rumors about Jack have been going around forever, but none of us have ever seen anything that proves that he is gay." (Dr. Jensen did socialize with Jack Wahl occasionally and would know more about Jack's social life than Dave Watkin.)

Agent Latozke seemed to support the theory about Jack's lifestyle from the investigation's beginning, and added, "We've been called to Jack's house quite often. Sometimes he goes a bit overboard. He's been getting worse, coming on stronger. There's been a big change the last few months." Agent Latozke did not elaborate in the investigation notes, but the group just seemed to accept his analysis.

Dr. Watkin suggested that the investigators talk with Gary Shannon and John Bergman from Hoople, North Dakota, since they were well-known homosexuals who lived in the area. Again, I found it hard to believe that Dave Watkin inserted himself as an expert on the homosexual community, but his comments were documented in the investigation reports.

BCI Special Agent David Lybeck included the following in his investigation notes: "Witnesses interviewed have also advised us and there is evidence that Dr. Wahl is a homosexual." I believe this group of witnesses included the group from Stu's Pub who were interviewed on Thursday, February 13, 1986.

To me, it seems like the officers should have followed up on any and all leads to solve the case. Instead, they *only* followed the idea that Jack's murder was a crime of passion, related to his homosexuality. They were not open-minded.

Another Theory

My brother-in-law Mark had been recently diagnosed with a medical condition. He did not take his medication regularly and liked to drink and party a lot, thus his disease was not managed well. This was a problem since he was licensed to drive a car.

The week of the murder, Mark had an accident at the main intersection in downtown Cavalier. There was only one car involved in the accident, since Mark hit a telephone pole. Since the family owned a car dealership, a wrecker was called, and the damaged car was hidden at the dealership. The Gregory family knew that it would be a real problem for Mark if anyone learned that he had a medical event while driving. When Jack learned of the incident, he immediately referred Mark to a neurology specialist in Fargo to conduct tests to determine whether his condition was a factor in the car accident.

The following day, Dr. David Watkin came to my office at the hospital and threatened me. This physician told me that if my friend Jack had covered for my brother-in-law by hiding his diagnosis, he'd sue my family for everything we had and ruin Jack too. He threatened to file a report with the medical licensing board.

Jack tolerated Dave Watkin at work but never invited him to social events. The only relationship the two doctors had was professional and clinic related. Dr. Watkin was the only physician partner who had never been invited to Dr. Wahl's home. More, he and his wife didn't socialize with the other physicians at all.

On Tuesday night, February 11, 1986, Jack called me at home to tell me that he and Dr. Watkin had been arguing over Mark's hospital medical record. I told Jack about the incident with the same doctor in my office earlier that day. Jack was furious.

Two days later, Jack was the victim of a homicide. Two weeks later, I contacted Sonny, the BCI investigator, and told him this story. I thought it might be related to the murder due to the timing. I was never contacted for follow-up questions, so I always assumed that Sonny simply dismissed my story. After all, I was a female. What would I know about Jack's lifestyle!

Interviews

Several young, local men were in Stu's Pub the night of Wednesday, February 12, 1986. All of them were interviewed the next day by Pembina County Deputy Sheriff Alan Latozke. Most of them reported that they had gone to Stu's after bowling next door at Sammy's. Only Art Snell was seated at the bar when Jack Wahl entered Stu's. The two talked from their separate locations, according to bartender Julie Young.

Each of the young men at Stu's was asked if they knew about parties at Dr. Wahl's house, and they all acknowledged knowing that it was common for Dr. Wahl to let the bar customers know if there would be a party at his house when the bar closed. The young customers at Stu's Pub were aware of the rumors of Jack's homosexuality, and mentioned that they would never go to his house alone, due to the rumors. It didn't appear that anyone was ever excluded from this invitation, but there was no party planned for that late Wednesday night. This was confirmed by Julie Young, who also reported that Jack Wahl left the bar alone around 1:00 a.m.

Jack was seen driving around Cavalier after 1:00, according to the sheriff's report, two unidentified witnesses, and Cavalier Police Chief Johnny Reynolds. It should be noted that Jack always drove unique cars in flashy colors that were easily identified.

In the days following the murder, many of our friends were also brought in for questioning. Initially, these targeted individuals were added to a list compiled by local law enforcement as potential murderers, because they fit the gay theory. Mark Gregory, my brother-in-law was questioned as part of this group, as was Kenny our gardener, and our friend Jim, the pharmacist. All three men reported to the investigators that Jack Wahl had never approached them in a sexual way.[11] They also reported that Jack was like a family member to each of them.

When they were questioned, Mark, Kenny, and Jim all told the authorities that I would know some answers to their questions, since I was a good friend and spent a lot of time with Jack. (This is documented in the investigation notes.)

How I wish the police had taken their suggestions, but I was never questioned after the murder. From my perspective, there was good reason to challenge the gay theory. First and foremost, I had personal knowledge about Jack and about many of his routines and habits. I had helped Jack move into his new house in 1980, along with some other close friends. My role had been to organize the kitchen and closets. Later, when I hosted parties with Jack, I knew where everything was, and I likely would have noticed if any things were missing.

I also could have disputed one of the rumors about boxes of pornographic materials stored behind the bar in the lower-level family room. I know that Jack sent me to that storeroom many times, and I never saw anything other than liquor there. He also never asked me to stay out of that storeroom.

Of course, this information didn't fit the police narrative. If this was a gay revenge murder, what would a woman know about it? Since local law enforcement focused on the idea that Jack was gay, and that this was the reason for the violence, I don't think they thought I would have any knowledge related to the murder.

Kenny Askew

Kenny was still in high school when he came to work as our gardener. Many people hired high school kids to mow their lawns, but Kenny was so much more to us than that. He planted and cared for our plants and flowers and was always available to help us with other household projects. We truly loved him and needed him!

Behind our house, we had a large, tiered rock garden, compliments of the previous owners. It was filled with perennials, berries, and seasonal plants. It never looked better than when Kenny was caring

Kenny Askew and "Baby" Jack mowing our lawn.

for it. He also mowed and trimmed the yard weekly, and at Christmastime he put the lights on our trees. He wrapped the Christmas lights around each branch of the evergreen tree by our front door. He told me once that there were 10,000 white lights on that one tree! Kenny was amazing.

Thank God Kenny was so dedicated! As time went on, Kenny became another member of our family, attending all the family events, including the births of both kids. Jack, Kenny, and I all had June birthdays, and we often celebrated together. Jack also hired Kenny as his gardener.

In his interview, Kenny offered that Jack had been seen with another of the local young men—Matt Hughes. Matt Hughes also had periodic run-ins with the local cops, so Kenny thought it was strange that Jack would be with him. Kenny offered Matt Hughes as a potential suspect, but Matt Hughes was not interviewed as far as I know. Kenny's interview was brief and undated.[12]

The Gregory family owned a speed boat, and we liked to water ski on the nearby Icelandic Park's Renwick Lake during the summer. Kenny became an avid skier and was usually with us at the lake. As time went by, Kenny usually went to my parents' lake cabin in central Minnesota with us too. Mike needed his skiing buddy nearby, since I was busy with the kids.

It wasn't much of a surprise when, after high school, Kenny bought the local greenhouse.

Kenny, Mike, and the kids preparing to ski.

He was also good at flower arrangements and did very well. Everyone liked him. Eventually he decided to go to college and left Cavalier. We have kept in touch all these years later.

As an adult, Kenny came out and let his extended family and friends know that he was gay. (This really wasn't much of a surprise.) He now lives in Minneapolis where he has a great job. We often visit him there, and he still comes to our family events. He has embraced a gay lifestyle and is very happy. At one time, Kenny dated another gay friend of mine, who I knew from Fargo.

Jim Salaba

Our friend Jim was a local pharmacist. In North Dakota, a pharmacist must own 51 percent of a drugstore or pharmacy. This limits the number of chain drugstores like Walgreens or CVS in the state. Unfortunately, just as Jim finished college in 1973, his dad, who owned a drug-store in Cavalier, died of cancer. Jim had taken a job in Washington State and was excited to begin his career out west where his sister lived. Instead, Jim had to return to his hometown and take over the family

Jim Salaba.

business. Jim moved in with his mother after his father died and still lived with Agnes at the time of the murder.

Jim and Jack were good friends, and they had dinner together Wednesday, February 12, 1986. As it turned out, it was Jack's last meal—and the last time Jim and Jack would enjoy their friendship. Jim, who was somewhat fragile anyway, was in shock after learning of the murder. He lived with his mother, but when the murder occurred, she was on the West Coast visiting her daughter. So Jim was home alone when he got the news about Jack.

Jim was also a high school friend of my husband, Mike. They grew up together in Cavalier, although Jim was a year older. Jim had been away at college when Jack Wahl moved to Cavalier in 1969, but met him later, through his parents. When Mike and I married, it was a natural progression to socialize with both Jim and his mother, Agnes. Jim liked to cook and entertain, and a group of us frequently had dinner at their house. He was famous for getting too drunk to serve dinner sometimes. We all drank too much.

Agnes Salaba always joined our group for drinks and dinner when Jim had people over to their home. Agnes was entertaining too, with her stories of days gone by, ancient

Jim and Agnes Salaba.

gossip, and local romances. We all enjoyed her. None of the friends envied Jim, though. He was basically with his mother all day at the drugstore, where she helped with the bookkeeping, and all night at home.

Remember the fictional small town of Mayberry, featured in the 1968-1971 CBS television series starring Andy Griffith? Sheriff Andy Taylor of Mayberry lived with his mother, Aunt Bee, who could be a stand-in for Agnes Salaba personality-wise. (They were about the same size and shape, too.)

Jim Salaba was active in a local theatre group. A talented actor, he could sing too. This was an interesting phenomenon, because at work in the drugstore, he was very shy. On stage, Jim was a totally different person.

Jim had talked to close friends about being gay. Unfortunately in his situation—living in a small town with his mother—it was difficult to live a gay lifestyle. In addition, it was difficult for Jim to take vacations, since he had to pay a relief pharmacist while he was away from the drugstore, and that was expensive. Sometimes, his sister who was also a pharmacist would come to help relieve Jim at the drugstore so he could get away for a break.

During Jim's interview with the investigators on February 14, 1986, he denied being gay. He also noted that Jack Wahl was like an older brother to him, and "he emphatically denied" ever having a sexual interest in Jack. He said as well that Jack never approached him with a physical advance.

Later, Jim told investigators that his mother usually accompanied him when he visited Jack's home, and that Mike and I were often included in the group at Jack's house. Jim also explained that Jack was his father's doctor, and that they were great friends when he was still alive. Jim got to know him when he returned to Cavalier in 1973, after he graduated from college.

During the investigation, Jim described a party at Jack's house when Charlie Kippen and Don Currie, a local banker, got into a fight. Jim admitted that he had been to a few parties late at night at Jack's. I also remember that Jim had talked about being at Jack's when Jim O'Rourke had stopped by on his way to Langdon. Jim Salaba didn't like Jim O'Rourke much. He thought he was mean.

Jean Speckman

The night of the murder, Jim Salaba and Jean, a local widow in Agnes Salaba's age group, had dinner at the Cedar Inn with Jack. This wasn't unusual. Jack had dinner with lots of different people. It was so much better than eating alone!

Jean's husband had died the year Jack came to Cavalier. Jean was suddenly alone, so they frequently had dinner together. Jean would usually make a hot dish (a casserole) when Jack was coming to her house. Jack enjoyed Jean's boisterous company and always included her in the large gatherings he eventually hosted at his new home.[13]

Jean was interviewed by Pembina County Deputy Sheriff Latozke in her home at noon, February 13, 1986.

She reported that Jack and Jim had come to her house for drinks at 7:15 p.m. that Wednesday. They later went to the Cedar Inn Steakhouse and Lounge, where they had dinner and drinks, and left around 11:00 p.m. As they were leaving, Jean said that she'd never been to Salaba's home, and the three friends decided to stop there for a night cap and a tour.

At midnight, Jack took Jean back to her house and said good night. Jack mentioned that he had a busy day tomorrow (Thursday), but instead Jack proceeded on to Stu's Pub for one more night cap. He wasn't ready to spend the rest of the night alone, although, according to the bartender at Stu's, he sat alone at the bar. There were some regulars in the bar and several people who were shooting pool.

Jim Salaba was one of the last people to see Jack alive, and since local law enforcement had made the assumption that Jim was gay, he was one of the first people interviewed by Dave Lybeck, a BCI investigator, and Pembina County Deputy Sheriff Joe Martindale, when the investigation began the next day.

The night after he was interviewed by the investigation team, Agnes called and asked me and another friend to go and check on Jim, since he wasn't answering her telephone calls. When we arrived at the Salaba house, Jim was in a bad way. He was drunk and threatening suicide, and of course he had access to a variety of medications if he had wanted to overdose. We spent the night talking him out of suicide and calling his mother with updates.

Years later, after Agnes died, Jim finally moved to the state of Washington, where he lives with a gay partner, works for a chain pharmacy, and acts in local theatre. He is semi-retired.

John Nelson

I don't know whether John Nelson was gay, and it was never implied in the news reports. The media did report that John Nelson was in Stu's Pub on Wednesday night, shooting pool with friends. Jack was there too, but they were not together.

John Nelson was scheduled for a polygraph or lie detector test on March 10, 1986, along with fifteen other locals, according to Pembina County Sheriff Wells who had returned from his vacation. John Nelson admitted that he had been to Wahl's house on previous occasions, and he voluntarily provided his fingerprints. I was not given access to his interview notes.

Suicide

John Nelson worked in the family's construction business and lived at home with his parents. The Nelson family had previously experienced tragedy. Bill Nelson, John's brother, had died in a car fire eight years earlier.

On the evening of March 11, 1986, the day after his lie detector test, John Nelson called a friend to talk. The conversation ended around midnight, when John Nelson suddenly shot himself in his parents' basement.

Nelson's family described him as a gentle, loving son, unable to commit a violent crime. The Nelson family shared his suicide note with the *Grand Forks Herald*:[14]

Dear Mom & Dad,

I love you both very much. You've given me a very good life. I've had good friends and great family, but I've never been really happy. I almost tried suicide, but my friend Teddy stopped me. I wish I could explain why, but I can't. Ever since Bill died I've felt responsible. The police think I killed Dr. Wahl, and somehow I feel responsible for that, even though I didn't do it. Tell everyone in the family I love them and all my friends that I'll miss them. I hope God can forgive me for what I'm doing and I hope you can forgive me, too.

Love, John

Dorothy Wahl, Jack's mother, mentioned this second tragedy in a personal note to me, saying, "I got to have my son twice as long as Mrs. Nelson."

Dr. Maxine Rasmussen, a Grand Forks-based psychologist who saw patients in the Cavalier Clinic every Thursday, agreed that if someone was going to commit suicide, they would most likely want to "clear their chest." In other words, confess. John Nelson's letter to his family did not include a confession.

I knew Dr. Maxine Rasmussen through our mutual friend, Jack. We often got together for social events in both Cavalier and Grand Forks. In fact, the three of us had dinner at the Cedar

Maxine Rasmussen.

Inn and drinks at Jack's house the week prior to the murder.

Dr. Rasmussen described the potential murderer for the *Grand Forks Herald* as, "A borderline personality, someone who wants his own way and has strong feelings." She added, "It was not sex-related."[15] She also described the general personality of a murderer: "The murderer would be immature, self-centered, demanding and impulsive, have a short fuse, and strong feelings."

Dean Becker

In a review of the investigation notes, it was immediately clear that the Pembina County sheriff had decided that Jack was gay and that he partied too much. One of the interviews that solidified this framework was the one with Dean Becker.

Dean told the investigators that he and John Nelson had frequented Jack's after-hours parties, including spending time with Jack, naked in his oversized tub with jets. According to Dean, at one of these events, Jack grabbed John Nelson in his crotch. John was offended by this and saw it as a sexual attack. According to Dean, this event occurred about a year prior to the murder.[16]

Becker said for the next year or so, John Nelson vacillated between thoughts of blackmailing Jack and of killing "the son-of-a-bitch." John Nelson wanted to purchase a bar in nearby Edinburg, North Dakota, and thought Dr. Wahl might be willing to invest $70,000 to buy it. After the attack, John felt he might have some leverage. This scenario fit perfectly into the investigator's theory. I wouldn't have put much confidence in Dean's story, because I didn't know him as someone who was trustworthy, but the authorities appeared to credit his story. It's not clear if Dean Becker approached the authorities, or if they contacted him. The notes are labeled as a "statement" rather than an interview.

In the discussion with BCI investigator Sonny Dump, Dean Becker was asked if he and John Nelson owned knives. Becker replied that they had bought knives together about eight or nine years ago when they were teenagers. According to Dean Becker, the knife John bought had a plastic handle and was extra-long, "The main part of John's knife with the blade closed was five or six inches long." Dean's knife was shorter and had a wooden handle.

In a July 1986 interview, Pembina County Sheriff Glenn Wells told the *Grand Forks Herald* that there was only one person involved in the crime. In December 1986, just prior to his retirement, Sheriff Wells stated that the last person to see Jack alive was now dead. The community assumed that this meant that John Nelson killed Dr. Wahl.

John Nelson killed himself in his parents' basement after he was interviewed by the Pembina County investigators. Dean Becker was killed in an ATV accident in 2018, while driving on a country road north of Cavalier. (He was not wearing a helmet when he was ejected.) The murder investigation may have had a different result if these two locals had lived longer. I know that I would like to question them!

John Nelson's parents have continued to live in the Cavalier community. I'm sure they still wonder if their son was responsible for Dr. Wahl's death. I hope they have supportive friends and family.

Other Stories

Included in the notes from the murder investigation was a report from BCI Special Agent Lybeck. He stated that a call had been received at the Pembina County Sheriff's Office on February 14, 1986, from the sheriff's office at Rugby, North Dakota. The report explained that a young man, Carey Peltier from Cavalier, had stopped and asked for fuel assistance around noon. Peltier, who was known for carrying knives by the Cavalier-based police and sheriff's departments, was traveling with a passenger to Minot, North Dakota. The Ramsey County sheriff wanted to inform the Pembina County investigators about this incident, in case it was related to the reported homicide the previous night.

Another strange, but probably unrelated, event took place the same night that Dr. Wahl was murdered. In fact, this story appeared on the front page of the *Cavalier Chronicle* on Tuesday, February 18, 1986, next to the story about the murder. The following summary, paraphrases the news story:

- Headline—"Skeleton Found After Fire Near Osnabrock" (North Dakota)
- The victim's remains were found after a fire destroyed a rural and vacant home early Wednesday morning (February 12, 1986).

- An autopsy was not possible due to the condition of the body.
- The victim was a thirty-two-year-old registered nurse, Chari Dalsted, who worked at the Cavalier County Hospital in Langdon, North Dakota.
- The destroyed home was owned by her grandmother, Violet Ward of Langdon, North Dakota.
- The North Dakota Bureau of Criminal Investigations (BCI) and the Cavalier County Sheriff's Office will continue the investigation.

Initially, there was some speculation that these two unattended deaths from the same area were connected. I don't remember hearing any follow-up information on Chari Dalsted's death, so I can only assume that the investigators didn't find any links between the two untimely deaths.

More Notes from the Investigation

As part of the investigation, three beer cans were taken into evidence from Jack's basement family room. According to Pembina County Sheriff Glenn Wells, John Nelson's prints were identified on two cans of Miller Lite beer, and Jack's fingerprints were found on a can of Coors beer, on the coffee table near the body. Dr. Larson verified that Jack drank Coors when he drank beer and that the NOW cigarette butts in the ashtray were probably Jack's, because he smoked that brand. The housekeeper had commented in a newspaper report that she didn't clean downstairs unless Dr. Wahl specifically requested it, so the beer cans could have been from a previous gathering.

Dr. Tareen remembered that he had asked to borrow a medical book from Jack recently, and that Jack had responded that he hadn't been downstairs for three weeks, but he'd look in the basement and see if he could find it.

Deputy Sheriff Martindale reported that tire tracks on the south side of Jack's driveway matched the tires on John Nelson's Trans Am. (There weren't a lot of places to buy tires in Cavalier, so I would guess that many local cars would feature the same tires.) It was February, so it was easy to track tire prints in the snow. At the time of the murder, there were no houses across the street from Jack's house. Instead, the empty lot would have probably been piled with snow from the plows cleaning the street. There were no neighbors across the street who could monitor the activities at Jack's house.

Jack's car was in his garage. Sonny Dump, the BCI special agent, also noted that he photographed a tennis shoe print on the cement garage floor. It was located on the passenger side of the car. It doesn't appear that this clue was followed at all.

11. Law and Order

The FBI

T HE FBI WAS NEVER INVOLVED in the investigation
of Jack's death, with the exception of some lab
assistance. This case didn't meet the criteria for their
involvement.[17] One of the criteria for FBI involvement
is if the crime suspect crossed state borders. Obviously,
the investigators didn't believe that whoever killed Jack
left the state after the murder, although the Minnesota
border was less than twenty miles east of Cavalier,
and the Manitoba border and the nearest crossing to
Canada was at Neche, North Dakota, fewer than twenty
miles north of Cavalier.

According to FBI reports and Pew Research, one
third of all murders in the US are never solved. FBI
reports also accept the fact that there is little likelihood
of a case being solved if there is no evidence found
within the first seventy-two hours. As a result, most of
the crimes reported in the US don't end with an arrest,
charging someone with a crime, or prosecution.

The FBI's clearance rate data relies on information voluntarily reported by local law enforcement
agencies around the country, but not all departments

participate. In addition, a crime reported in one year, might be cleared in a future year. Some cases are closed through "exceptional means," when the suspect dies before they can be charged or appear in court.

There is also a significant variation in reporting and solving crimes, depending on the offense. For example, in 2015, 61.5 percent of the murders cleared by police also included non-negligent manslaughter.

State's Attorney

In February 1986, when the case was new, newspaper reports described the investigation being conducted by the Pembina County Sheriff's office (Glenn Wells, Joe Martindale); the North Dakota Bureau of Criminal Investigations (E. F. "Sonny" Dump); and, the Cavalier Police Department (John Reynolds). None of these officers is alive today.

Bob Lee was the state's attorney for Pembina County, and as such took the lead in criminal cases. In North Dakota, each county has an elected state's attorney, who is a county employee. They don't report to the North Dakota attorney general. Instead, law enforcement employees like the BCI investigators report to the attorney general, to provide a "check and balance" on the legal system. The office of the attorney general *can* provide some support to both investigation teams and the legal representatives if requested, but any advice would primarily focus on interpreting North Dakota laws.

The state's attorney role includes serving as the legal counsel and advisor to each county in the state, and often being called on to interpret the meaning of North Dakota Century Code (laws and legislation). In 1986, Bob Lee was the Pembina County state's attorney, thus he was the lead on the Wahl murder case.

An April 1986 newspaper report described the results of the autopsy and said that evidence from the crime scene was still being studied. Pembina County State's Attorney Bob Lee was quoted as saying, "The autopsy results don't change the focus of the investigation or reveal any surprises. Nothing has changed." There was no sign of a struggle or forced entry, and it didn't appear that anything was missing, so robbery was not considered a motive for the crime.

By July, the *Grand Forks Herald* announced that the FBI reports from Washington and the State Crime Lab in Bismarck had been sent to the Pembina County investigators, indicating that the crime lab's work was completed.

Bob Lee was accused of "dragging his feet" because he didn't release any information to the media. He told reporters that he would issue weekly press releases in a February 1986 interview, but had only issued one by mid-October:[18]

> *Contrary to recent media reports, the investigation into the death of Dr. John D. Wahl has not been completed. My office has requested of the investigating agencies that there be additional investigation and follow-up into certain aspects of the case. Upon completion of the investigation to my satisfaction, a decision will be made based on all the available evidence as to what action will be pursued.*

Bob Lee reported that he had two options: (1) to call for an inquest by either the state's attorney or the county coroner; or (2) to ask the district court judge to impanel a grand jury. Lee favored calling a grand jury.

So what is a grand jury? Here is what I have learned:

- A grand jury is a legal body empowered to review potential criminal conduct and determine whether criminal charges should be brought. It may compel witnesses and share documents separate from the courts, since the courts do not preside over a grand jury.
- A grand jury usually has twenty-three members who are selected at random through voter rolls and motor vehicle registrations, and who examine an accusation prior to a trial.
- A grand jury decides whether someone should be *charged*; a trial decides whether someone is *guilty*.
- A grand jury only needs probable cause to return an indictment; a trial jury must have proof beyond a reasonable doubt to find someone guilty.
- An *indictment* is an accusation of *probable cause* that a crime was committed; it does not require evidence of a crime.
- The purpose of the grand jury is not to determine guilt or innocence.
- The grand jury operates in secrecy.

- The prosecutor impanels a group of people to examine evidence and decide if an indictment should be brought against an individual.
- The prosecutor may subpoena witnesses and documents, and put them under oath.
- A super majority or 60 percent is required for an indictment; e.g., 14/23.
- The preponderance of the evidence is considered for "proof."
- Jury selection is also called *voir dire*.

District Court

District Court was located in Grafton, North Dakota, approximately forty-five miles from Cavalier. Judge James O'Keefe was in charge of the North East Judicial District Court. He described the cost of a grand jury hearing to taxpayers and the time it would take to review the evidence, and then added that he couldn't charge a dead person with a crime anyway. Like the investigators, Judge O'Keefe believed that John Nelson was the murderer from the evidence he had reviewed.[19] He probably also considered how difficult it would be to find an objective jury. Jack Wahl was a popular doctor who had hundreds of loyal patients in the region. And there were the months of gossip. It would be difficult to keep potential jurors from talking about the court discussions.

In addition to a grand jury hearing, two other legal strategies into the murder investigation could have included a *coroner's inquest* or a *probable cause hearing*. The coroner's inquest is usually requested when the death is sudden or unexplained. A probable cause hearing uses a warrant for an arrest of a suspect or a search warrant to determine whether there is sufficient evidence to charge someone with a crime. Neither of these tactics was pursued.

Bob Lee was up for reelection for his fourth term as Pembina County state's attorney, but by October 1986, he cited personal reasons for not running again. Glenn Wells, Pembina County sheriff, favored Lee's opponent, Laurie Cook (Fontaine) another local attorney, and everyone in town knew it. It didn't help that Bob Lee was reluctant to speak to the media regarding the Wahl murder investigation.

Bob Lee was not originally from Cavalier or Pembina County. (He was from my hometown, Wahpeton, North Dakota.) I had learned that "once an outsider, always an outsider" firsthand. My in-laws had lived in Cavalier since 1959, and people still referred to them as "coming from Crookston, Minnesota." Assimilation and acceptance in a small community takes a really long time! Since Bob Lee wasn't a "local" he didn't have a built-in support system. People weren't happy with the way the investigation had been run, primarily because he didn't share information on the case, as he had promised when the investigation began.

Ultimately, before October ended, State's Attorney Bob Lee sent a letter to the editor of the *Cavalier Chronicle*, stating "My office has not received evidence sufficient to warrant the institution of criminal proceedings against any one person. I will return the case to the investigative agencies."[20]

More Rumors

Thanks in part to the slow grind of the investigation and prosecution of Jack's case, rumors continued to grow throughout 1986. Local law enforcement officials certainly did not have much experience with high profile murder cases, so the case dragged on. Little information was released on any progress, so the citizens had to depend on the local grapevine for updates.

The *Cavalier Chronicle*, the local weekly newspaper, was published and distributed on Mondays, so local citizens had to wait a week for the "truth" to come out. In a small town, word-of-mouth versions of reality are common, and just like the "telephone game" many of us played as children, stories are modified with each individual communication.

When I moved to Cavalier in 1979, I often heard anecdotal stories about local (small-town) law enforcement. The stories were familiar to me, since I grew up in a small North Dakota community too. Most small towns had just one officer.

One of the local stories centered on Ed, a local policeman. According to the local folklore, Ed couldn't read or write. When he stopped someone for an infraction, the offender had to fill out their own ticket. Ed was able to position this technique as punishment, and got away with it for the fifteen years that he served as the Cavalier chief of police. Ed was retired at the time of the murder, but the current law enforcement officers were also closed-minded locals. They were not objective and had no experience with high-profile cases.

It seemed like the investigation had run its course. Judge O'Keefe refused to call a grand jury. Bob Lee was accused of having political motives. Glenn Wells was set to retire at the end of the year and had publicly stated, "There is only one person involved in the crime."

12. The Emotional Toll

Repercussions

W HEN A MURDER VICTIM IS killed with a gun, the murderer can be at a distance—across the room, for example. But when the victim is stabbed to death, the murderer is in close proximity—physically touching the victim while taking his life. When the murder is never solved, it just adds to the anguish and the doubts. Is the murderer living nearby? Do I know the murderer?

I still cringe when a stabbing is portrayed on television or in a movie. When you've lost someone through a murder, whether it's a friend, a sibling, or a spouse, it is difficult to separate personal feelings from a fictitious portrayal. It is always worse when the story is based on true-crime stories, like the television shows *Dateline* or *2020*.

Across the US, four out of ten homicides are never solved. My friend's murder is one of 269,205 cold cases in the US as of December 2019. Some jurisdictions describe a cold case as an unsolved murder that is more than one year old. In Oregon, a cold case is defined as "a homicide or murder that has been thoroughly investigated with all leads exhausted, yet it remains unsolved."

Six thousand cases are added to the list of unsolved homicides every year in the US. In 2016, there were 15,556 homicides reported and 6,316 cases have gone "cold." There were only 9,240 arrests for these homicides.[21] This fact is much more meaningful when someone you know is included in the data.

Definitely Murder

It's ironic that Jack avoided service during the Vietnam War and then was murdered in his own home in a small community where most people never locked their doors. Cavalier residents felt safe; that is until February 13, 1986.

I realize that there can be solid reasons for killing another person. I know if I was in jeopardy, I'd fight like hell until the end! When it's a soldier deep in the Vietnam jungle or on a sandy mountain top in Iraq, who must make the split-second decision to kill in order to live, there is no question about how one must react. But to kill someone in their own home, where they felt safe?

My friend Jack had fallen asleep or passed out from a night of drinking. He was stabbed to death on his couch. The murderer reached over the back of the sectional couch and stabbed him with some type of knife six times. He was defenseless. He didn't react or fight back. According to the local investigators, nothing in his home was out of order. And according to police reports, there was no struggle. Other than anger, there doesn't appear to be a motive for the murder.

Surviving

The first time I went anywhere after the murder, I took my son Jack to the 1961 Walt Disney movie *101 Dalmatians*, at the local movie theatre. Jack was almost three years old. The movie had recently been rereleased. This was an animated movie, or a cartoon, with Cruella DeVille as the antagonist.

In the movie, the family's two Dalmatian dogs had fifteen puppies. Cruella wanted to buy them to make a fur coat. When Cruella and her henchmen pulled out their knives to kill the puppies, I lost it and began to cry. I had to leave the movie theater.

Since the murder in 1986, I have responded this way whenever knives are used to terrorize or kill someone in a movie, a book, or a TV program. I always have a visceral reaction. I also think about evidence like lip prints on a glass or a strange hair where it doesn't belong. I have always wondered if this is a form of post-traumatic stress, or PTSD.

I still react to an unsolved murder whether it is in the news or in a movie, and find it difficult to watch a violent movie or television show, especially if knives are involved. I guess you could say that I continue to be victimized by a crime that happened to my friend thirty-five years ago.

The National Sheriff's Association released a research report in August 2011 called "Survivors of

Homicide Victims." One of the findings was, "Survivor pain is the same whether the case is solved or not." I don't agree. If the case was solved, it would provide some measure of closure. I've read many documents regarding survivor grief, and they usually say that it helps to know what happened, or to hear that there was an arrest, but the reality is your loved one is still gone forever, and you didn't get to say good-bye. One of my regrets is that I never told my friend Jack how much he meant to me, and then he was gone. Let your friends and family know how valuable they are before it is too late.

The trauma of my friend's unsolved murder affected the *entire* community, of course, not just me. In my case, I was depressed, but I still had to go to work at the hospital and take care of my kids.

Sad

If Jack had been a relative, instead of *just* a friend, I would have been included in the discussions with law enforcement as part of the investigation, but as a friend, I was powerless. On the other hand, I have always felt responsible for identifying the motive and the murderer. I don't know why, except that there have been so many strange encounters with many different people over the past thirty-five years that I haven't been able to forget that day.

I guess you could call it a gut feeling. I think that the investigators had a myopic view of the murder. Dean Becker had described the situation with John Nelson to perfectly align with what Sheriff Wells had already hypothesized. I don't remember Dean Becker as someone to be trusted. He had a reputation for drinking too much and was not dependable. I knew him from the time he worked at the local nursing home. John Nelson was dead and couldn't defend himself, so the sheriff basically just agreed with Becker's description.

The murder was brutal and the murderer was probably someone Jack knew. I don't think the primary motive was gay rage, as the police seemed to think. Instead, my theory is that the murderer's motivation was control of Jack's extensive art collection. In my thinking, the gay issue was secondary.

The Will

Attorney Argue (such a great name for a lawyer) had prepared Jack's will in 1984. We learned after the funerals that, as expected, Jack's family members were the beneficiaries. Jack's brother Richard was named executor of the will. He was the youngest member of the family, at age thirty. Jack's three sisters ranged in age from thirty-two to forty at the time of the murder. The oldest of the sisters was already a widow, and received half of the estate. The remaining assets were distributed between the other siblings as dictated through Jack's will.

The probate documents describe a separate appraisal and itemized listing of Jack's art collection, which was valued at approximately $32,000 in 1986. The appraised value would be around $75,000 in today's dollars. Jack's friend, Jim O'Rourke was responsible for the final inventory and appraisal. The probate documents don't describe any distribution.

In March 1986, following the initial investigation, the house was turned over to Jack's family. Eventually it was sold to Jack and Pauline Page, friends of Jack's who already lived nearby on a small acreage south of Cavalier on Highway 18.

Jack and Pauline Page were good friends with Jack and often traveled with him. When Jack Page was diagnosed with cancer, Jack flew to California, brought his chemotherapy medicine to him, and administered the treatment in their home. I could never understand how the Pages were able to live in a home where their friend was murdered and where they often socialized. I was never able to enter Jack's house after the murder.

Grieving

We've all heard of the Kübler-Ross model of grief (1969), also known as the five responses to loss. The stages are: (1) denial; (2) anger; (3) bargaining; (4) depression; and (5) acceptance. As you read my story, you will recognize the classic grieving process. I know that I'm no different from others who have experienced a sudden loss. Writing this book is my way of reaching Stage 5, and it's taken me thirty-five years to get to this point.

The days between the discovery of the murder and the memorial service in Cavalier and the funeral in Jack's hometown, are simply a blur. I was in *denial*.[22]

How could this happen in a small town to a person who was so respected by everyone in the community?

When you live in a rural, remote community, everyone is familiar in some way. You know the local residents through church or school or work or politics or through your children. Suddenly, you don't trust anyone. It's quite a change. I kept thinking that I would wake up and find out it was all a bad dream.

Anger

The *Grand Forks Herald*, the region's major newspaper, wasted no time getting to Cavalier and finding people who were willing to talk. After a few days, I couldn't take the innuendos and agreed to talk to the reporters, along with my friend Dr. Maxine Rasmussen. I felt like Maxine and I really knew Jack as a person, rather than as a physician or closet homosexual. Others preferred to talk only about his lifestyle.

One of my quotes that appeared in a lengthy article in the *Herald* focused on Jack's loneliness.[23] Several other people were quoted too, including Dr. Rasmussen and Jack's uncle, Arvid Benson from Moorhead.

Eventually, the editor of the *Herald* scheduled a town hall meeting at a Cavalier restaurant so that everyone could talk directly to the citizens of the region through the newspaper. A lot of backlash had occurred by then, including letters to the editor complaining about the tone of the *Herald's* reports.

I was *angry* with the newspaper, and I wasn't the only one, as demonstrated through the letters to the editor from 1986. Wes Argue, a respected Pembina County attorney and owner of the Hamilton Bank, was one of the citizens who wrote to the *Grand Forks Herald*:[24]

> The Herald *has managed to anger an entire community, and upset an already bereaved family, and upset me enough to write. Your story about Dr. John D. Wahl's murder . . . contained accounts of his personal life that were totally uncalled for . . . you made it a fourth-rate account by adding gossip that had no bearing on the news story . . . the facts, if they were indeed facts, were totally irrelevant . . . you have angered Dr. Wahl's friends in the Cavalier community. . . .*

Next, the electronic media came to town! Just like portrayals on TV and in popular movies, the television reporters were aggressive, shoving cameras in the mourners' faces and shouting questions at the memorial service at the funeral home in Cavalier, and then again at the small country church where the funeral and burial were held.

I just wanted to go to sleep and wake up with my world back to "normal." During this time, many people sent us sympathy cards with very thoughtful notes. I was surprised that so many people knew that Jack was like a family member.

I also knew that eventually I'd have to go back to work at the hospital and that Jack would no longer be stopping by my office. To cope with the sudden loss, we drank a lot, reminisced about the good times, and tried to figure out who murdered our friend.

After Jack's funeral, a coworker said to me, "You were so lucky to have a friend like Jack for thirteen years. Some people never have close friends."

Depression and Bargaining

One month after the funeral, I learned I was pregnant with our second child. I was *depressed* during the entire pregnancy—not because I was pregnant, but because of our loss and the uncertainty surrounding the murder investigation.

In the 1980s, it was still considered okay to have a glass of wine when you were pregnant. Smoking was discouraged, but the pregnancy guidelines weren't as strict as they are today. Dr. Larson told me that when his generation was having children in the '50s and '60s, "We all drank booze and smoked cigarettes, and there wasn't an entire generation of addicted children with birth defects."

I had been drunk every day for a month. The doctor downplayed my confession, but that's when I started *bargaining*: "Please, let my baby be normal!" I only gained nineteen pounds during the pregnancy. I was depressed and couldn't eat. When she arrived in October, my daughter weighed six pounds, fifteen ounces, which was a good weight. Whew!

Fall 1986

In September 1986, shortly before he was set to retire as the Pembina County sheriff, Glenn Wells suddenly appeared in my office at the hospital. He said, "I just have one question for you. Did Dr. Wahl have any Chicago Cutlery?"

I was so stunned by the sheriff's unscheduled appearance, and so mad that it had taken him eight months to ask me a question, that I replied, "Get the fuck out of my office!" I never talked with him again, and I didn't answer the question, either.

Chicago Cutlery was very popular in the 1980s. Most of the people who had a collection of these knives usually displayed them in a wooden block in their kitchens. The knives had wooden handles and carbon steel blades, and there were both steak knives and carving tools. Jack did own Chicago Cutlery, but I do not know if there were knives missing from his knife collection.

By late September 1986, the formal request for a grand jury was forwarded to the District Court by State's Attorney Bob Lee, and promptly denied by Judge O'Keefe. So when my daughter was born in October, the investigation had not made any progress.

In an article published by the *Grand Forks Herald*,[25] Pembina County State's Attorney Bob Lee reported he was not pursuing criminal proceedings against any person, due to insufficient evidence. The investigation had stalled, and Lee was accused of playing "political football," since he was up for reelection. I believe that the law enforcement officers had decided that John Nelson killed Jack as the result of a gay relationship, and Bob Lee, as the lead on the investigation for the state, didn't feel there was enough evidence. In addition, since Nelson was dead, he couldn't be charged, so the case would be in limbo anyway.

Becoming a Victim

Victim's Rights were primitive in 1986. *Marsy's Law* was eventually added to the North Dakota Century Code in 2016, granting victims of a crime certain rights. In the situation of my friend Jack, who was single and an adult, I'm not sure who would qualify as a victim in this situation—likely only his siblings and his parents.

Today, the National Institute of Justice recommends a "victim-centered and trauma-informed" approach to helping a victim's family and friends adjust to an unsolved murder, rape, or missing-person crime.[26]

An unsolved case might cause the victim's friends and family to live in fear of being retraumatized over time, because the perpetrator has eluded the criminal justice system or the case periodically reappears in news reports. I can testify that there is no closure for the victim's survivors.

Cold case investigators should understand and consider the psychological effects of simply not finalizing the outcome and its effect on the victim's friends and family—forever.

The loss of my friend Jack has never been resolved because the investigation has never officially ended.

As part of this writing project, I learned about a term coined in the 1970s by some college researchers: *ambiguous grief*. In my case, ambiguous grief is probably the best explanation for my internal struggle to make sense of this experience. According to the researchers, the main feature of ambiguous grief is that the loss is unclear or uncertain. It can lead to anxiety disorders like PTSD (post-traumatic stress disorder), depression, and/or unresolved grief. This loss impacts the victim's family, as well as coworkers and friends.

This new way of looking at grief was the result of the studies of Pauline Boss, PhD, and Hayley Hirschman, PhD, who began their research on grief and loss in the 1970s, following the Vietnam War.[27] They defined ambiguous grief as:

- Not a simple death or physical absence; remains unclear or uncertain in some way.
- A death or loss that is difficult to close because there is no official recognition of the loss.
- The loss can be either physical or psychological, as long as there is incongruence between absence/presence.

Examples of *physical absence with psychological presence* include: missing soldiers, people lost following storms and earthquakes, airplane explosions, kidnapped or missing children, or a family member who is in jail or in a nursing home. It can also describe the loss of a loved one who remains alive, but is "gone" due to dementia, a brain injury, or a stroke. I felt like this theory helped to explain my unending sense of loss.

I had a friend in Cavalier who had a nervous breakdown. She also suffered from post-partum depression. One day she told me, "I only see black and white. It's like a negative. Nothing is colored."

It wasn't until I moved back to Fargo in 1990 that I realized I had been living the same way—for years. My world view between the murder and leaving Cavalier was just like the negative view my friend described. I was as depressed as she was, I just wasn't medicated.

The last time I saw my friend Jack we were in the hospital lobby. He was wearing his usual faded-green scrubs. He walked through the door to the second floor, never to be seen again. The real story is that Jack was murdered later that night, and the case remains unsolved, thirty-five years later. The fact that he was *just a friend* makes my loss difficult to explain to others.

I can say now that Jack helped to keep me sane while I lived in Cavalier. He understood the difficult situation that I was in with the Gregory family, and he supported me. He was the only friend who really understood.

13. Leaving Cavalier

As I'VE SAID PREVIOUSLY, EVEN though I was married, I had total responsibility for our two children, since Mike never participated in any parenting activities. In addition, he didn't treat me with respect or have consideration for my needs or feelings. For example, after work, I would retrieve the kids from daycare at 4:30, but I still had to serve dinner at 5:00, so he could return to "work" by 6:00. The business stayed open every night until 9:00 p.m., although it was closed on Sunday.

Sometimes I would come out of the grocery store, and my car was gone. One of the Gregorys would have taken the car to show it to a customer. I had to search for dealer plates to find a car to drive home. The kids' car seats were usually just casually thrown in the back seat, so, I had to reinstall them too.

One time, I was leaving work and discovered that my car was gone and in its place was a pickup with a flat tire. I got in the pickup, and the janitor from work came over to tell me that I couldn't drive a vehicle that was sitting on a rim.

I replied, "Watch me. If *they* left me a vehicle that doesn't work, they deserve to have me drive it home as is." I chose the pronoun "they" because it could have been Mike, his brother, or their dad taking my vehicle and leaving the pickup with the flat tire. They all treated me the same way.

My Friend Jack

Since Jack understood the Gregory family dynamics so well, he was my support system. When he died, I felt like I was on my own with no one to talk to. I guess I did take Jack's friendship for granted. His death, though, became the catalyst to help me get on with my life.

By Christmas 1989, I'd had it with my life in Cavalier. My kids were three and seven, and I was basically a single parent, responsible for all their daily activities. Mike was either at work or with his brother at his dad's house.

After the murder, I was tired of living in a small town, and I filed for divorce in May 1990. I made plans to move back to Fargo. I was already living the life of a single mother with two kids, so I knew I could do it, and I had a broad network of friends in Fargo who would support me.

Two final incidents put me over the edge. First, my husband had told me all year that business was bad, and then utilized his year-end bonus to buy himself a Harley-Davidson motorcycle. Then, I asked him to pick up a toboggan I had purchased at the hardware store as a Christmas gift for the kids, and I came home after work to find it lying on the dining room floor.

Of course, I had the kids with me, and they saw their Christmas gift from Santa.

It brought home that with Jack gone, I didn't have anyone to talk to about family issues, as well as that my work and social life had changed too, especially since the case was never closed. Eventually, I realized that I just couldn't live the small-town life anymore. I would say that the murder was the catalyst to get me to make this big change. I hated my current life, but I finally felt ready to do something about it.

I told Mike that I needed some money, a car, and the kids, and that I planned to move to Fargo in August, so that Jack could start first grade in the local school system. I told him that he could keep the house and furnishings, because the kids would be spending time with him in Cavalier. He was incredulous that I would want to leave, and immediately launched a campaign to fight for custody of Jack and Sarah.

Others React

I called my mother in May 1990, to tell her that I was getting divorced and that it was my idea. Instead of offering unconditional love and support, she said, "My life was perfect, and you wrecked it. You better fix this." I guess she didn't want anyone to know that she had a child who was getting divorced. My parents' social standing in their small community took precedence over family life. (Note: My youngest brother has been divorced and remarried now, too!)

My friend and mentor, Dr. Frances Branchaud, a local retired optometrist who was in her 90s, offered to

Frances Branchaud and kids.

call my mother to support my decision to leave. Frances shared with me that she never appreciated Mike and remembered him as the unruly kid in her Catholic catechism class. She always told me that she couldn't believe I married him!

I originally met Frances through the Cavalier Catholic Church. She told me that she had outlived five of her seven children and that she had gone back to school to take over her husband's optometry practice when he died. She was a "tough cookie," and I loved her spirit!

So, between 1986 and 1990, my marriage had fallen apart, my best friend had been murdered, and my family was unsupportive. Thank God I had good friends in other places! Legal help would present another issue. Since I was leaving, and Mike was staying in Cavalier, I knew that I couldn't find a lawyer in town to represent me. I assumed that Mike would hire Neil Fleming. I found an attorney in Grand Forks, the nearest large city, eighty-five miles to the south of Cavalier.

When the lawyer strategized where to hold the hearing, I told him a story about my first encounter with Judge O'Keefe, when I was new in Cavalier and had been summoned to jury duty.

Judge O'Keefe

I had previously met Judge O'Keefe, the District Judge for Walsh and Pembina counties, when I had been called as a potential juror in a case involving Crystal Sugar, a large farmers' co-op with a manufacturing plant in nearby Drayton, North Dakota. As luck would have it, I wasn't included in the initial juror pool of twelve who were questioned. When the initial group was excused, I was brought up for questioning.

As I sat in the witness box by myself, the prosecuting and defense attorneys began to question me. Neil Fleming was the attorney for the owner whose land had been damaged by some run-off from the Crystal Sugar plant. The attorneys started the questioning with asking me where I was *from*—they knew that I wasn't a Pembina County native.

At one point, the judge started asking me questions too. One of the questions was, "Which one of the Gregory brothers are you married to?" They all seemed to want to know my entire history. I was so unnerved by the direct questioning that later I said it kept my marriage together for several more years. I didn't want to go back to a court room for any reason.

I remember that Neil Fleming told Judge O'Keefe that he had had an *open file* with the Gregory family for over twenty-five years. I didn't know what that meant at the time, but I later learned that he meant that he was the Gregory family attorney.

I wasn't chosen for jury duty, but from that time on, whenever Judge O'Keefe was in Cavalier for court, he would stop by my family's car dealership and say things like, "Which one of you is married to the blond?" This felt creepy as well as sexist, and I planned to avoid Judge O'Keefe at all costs.

After hearing this story, my Grand Forks attorney said: "Perfect. We're going to request a hearing in Grafton, in Judge O'Keefe's court room." My attorney thought that since the judge had previously met me, it would be an advantage. I had my doubts.

The divorce hearing was held on Halloween Day, 1990. I had already moved to Fargo with the kids in August. Judge O'Keefe asked me how I planned to manage the relationship with my ex-husband from two hundred miles away. I responded, "I can handle Mike." The judge took off his glasses, peered down at me from his bench, and replied, "I bet you can!"

My attorney was correct, and the divorce was finalized without difficulty.

I had always said that Cavalier was "world headquarters for male chauvinism," and I sure learned that when the community heard that I was leaving. Whispered comments included, "She doesn't know how good she's got it" and "Who does she think she is?"

Here's a great example of the chauvinism that was alive and well in Cavalier: after I relocated and settled in Fargo, I decided to move the kids' bank accounts to a Fargo bank, so that they could have the experience of saving money and going to a bank. I had established the accounts for Jack and Sarah, so my name was on the accounts as a joint owner. Mike was not involved in establishing the bank accounts, but his family owned stock in the bank. His name was never included on the kids' accounts. A couple of years after we divorced, I called the bank and asked to close the accounts and transfer the kids' accounts to a Fargo bank.

Within the hour of my call to the Cavalier bank, Mike called me and asked me "What are you up to, now?" I didn't know what he was referencing, but he soon accused me of taking the kids' money for myself. The bank president had called him and told Mike of my request to transfer the funds!

The Transition

Financially, there was nothing in my name from the marriage. The Gregorys were stockholders in the local bank but my name was never included on my husband's stock. I didn't even have my own savings account! The house wasn't in my name, and I drove a dealer car, so I didn't have any physical assets either.

Mike was a partner in the family business, but I knew better than to go after half of his share if I wanted to leave that year. I told my lawyer to ask for a cash payment, child support, and a car. Mike could have the house and furnishings. I just wanted to leave—with the kids.

The local hospital and nursing home where I worked were managed by a company with headquarters in Fargo, North Dakota. The management company provided a 401k as a retirement benefit. None of the local businesses, and of course none of the farm families, had benefits like we had working for the town's largest employer.

The best part of the retirement fund was that women didn't have to name their husbands on their retirement accounts in those days. We could also make changes without them signing off. I had $17,000 in that "get-away" fund, and I was getting a new life! It was the only asset I owned.

My attorney told me that I had to secure a job, find a place to live, and enroll the kids in school and daycare before we could go to court. Since I had lived in Fargo prior to moving to Cavalier, I had a lot of contacts there. On May 1, 1990, the divorce papers were served. On August 10, 1990, I moved to Fargo with the kids and the cat and started my next life.

On Halloween Day, October 31, 1990, I went to divorce court in Grafton, with the honorable Judge O'Keefe presiding. I remember being nervous about seeing Judge O'Keefe in court, since he had met me previously when I was called for jury duty, but the divorce was final when I left the courtroom that day and I had custody of the kids, which was my goal.

Coincidences

For readers who are unfamiliar with the Fargo-Moorhead Metro Area (MSA), it straddles two states and two counties, with four communities that share the metro. Fargo, North Dakota, is the largest city and Moorhead, Minnesota, shares the MSA on the Minnesota side of the Red River of the North. Dilworth,

Minnesota, and West Fargo, North Dakota, complete the metropolitan area. Today, there are approximately two hundred fifty thousand residents who live in the F-M Metro, with Fargo home to one hundred seventy-five thousand residents. Each community has its own school district and local government. I was required to stay in North Dakota as a result of my divorce agreement and found a town house in south Fargo, but I worked in Moorhead, Minnesota.

When I moved back to Fargo in 1990, I kept meeting people who had either a connection to Jack Wahl or to Cavalier. Others often asked me about the status of the four-year-old murder, because that's what they associated with Cavalier. I frequently saw Jack's cousin Kim, who was on the board of the senior housing project where I worked in Moorhead.

When I went to register my son for first grade at Lewis & Clark Elementary school, the principal asked me where we were moving from. When I said Cavalier, Roger Olgard immediately asked me if I knew Jack Wahl. Roger was from the same hometown and knew Jack from high school.

I will always be grateful for Roger Olgard's interest in my son, although I remember crying in the principal's office when this connection was made. It seemed that wherever I went, I would make a connection back to Jack. Even though I'd moved almost two hundred miles from Cavalier, the story of my friend Jack followed me.

In another situation, I decided to take my kids to see an art exhibit housed in a semi-trailer in our neighborhood. When we entered the trailer, the first painting I saw was one I recognized from Jack's collection. During the almost thirty years I lived in Fargo, I was never able to visit either the Plains Art Museum in Fargo or the Rourke Gallery in Moorhead, because I didn't want to risk seeing the familiar art from Jack's house in Cavalier.

I had a conversation with Dr. Joe Knutson, a retired Concordia College President, that took place just a few days before his death. I had gone to the Knutson home to discuss the possibility of Joe and his wife moving to an assisted living building where I worked. When I mentioned working on a previous assisted living project in Cavalier, Dr. Knutson had asked me if I knew Jack Wahl. There it was again!

According to Joe Knutson, who had retired from Concordia College in 1974, Jim O'Rourke and Jack knew each other through Concordia. Dr. Knutson told me that Jim was interested in having a gay relationship with Jack, but that Jack rebuffed his advances after leaving college. Again, I was surprised at all the connections. I was also surprised that Joe would know so much about Jim and Jack's relationship.

Dr. Knutson died suddenly on August 28, 1992, just two days after I visited him in his home. I remember that his death was front-page news in the *Forum*, and that when I saw that he had died, I realized that I wouldn't be able to follow up with all the questions I had after our brief visit.

I would also frequently run into Jim O'Rourke in restaurants and at other social activities in Fargo-Moorhead. When I would see him, I would remind him that I had previously known him through our mutual friend, Jack Wahl. He would rarely say anything, but he would always begin to sweat—a lot! (Perspiration would literally drip off his face and chin.)

I thought this strange, since I had spent a lot of time with Jim when he visited Jack in Cavalier, when they shared paintings for regional art shows. Looking back now, I think that Jack would invite me over to his house when Jim visited as some kind of "buffer" between them. If Dr. Knutson from Concordia was right, Jack might have wanted a third person at his house to prevent a confrontation with Jim.

Jim O'Rourke

Jim O'Rourke was born in 1933 in Langdon, North Dakota, just thirty-five miles from Cavalier, so he was often in the area. His parents, Joseph and Mildred Rourke, lived in Langdon until their deaths. Jim added the "O" to his name, but his two brothers didn't make that change.

Jim O'Rourke graduated from Concordia College in Moorhead in 1956, and served in the military in Europe. After Jim completed his military service, he returned to Moorhead and in 1960, established the Rourke Art Gallery with his brother Orland Rourke.

Jim O'Rourke was a small-framed guy who looked like a cross between Sherlock Holmes and a college professor. He was balding but wore his white hair long. He also had a bushy white mustache. He was usually dressed in a tie and a tweed sport coat when I would see him.

Jack had hung eleven of the paintings from his collection at our house, including a large one (42" x 66") that Jim O'Rourke had painted in 1966, called "Visby" (Red Church). Once, Jack brought Jim to our house to see the paintings there.

Jack had often told me not to tell anyone that I had his paintings, because if he "dropped dead," his brother would be the first one there to pick them up. When Jack died, Jim O'Rourke was the first person come to our house to collect Jack's paintings for an estate inventory. I was out of town at the time, and Mike handed the paintings to Jim with no questions asked.

I was able to keep a George Pfeifer painting that Jack had given us in 1979 as a wedding gift. Pfeifer was a regional artist who was well known to both Jim and Jack. I still own this art.

George Pfeifer was one of the many Concordia students who worked at the Rourke Gallery and took classes there. Later, he became well-known for his art in the region.

Another Sudden Ending

Jim O'Rourke fell in his home in 2011 and died, leaving his estate and art collection to the non-profit Rourke Art Gallery and Museum in Moorhead, Minnesota.

Some of the regional artists' works from Jim's art collection included: Charles Beck, Gordon Mortensen, Carl Oltvedt, George Pfeifer, Cyrus Running, Fritz Scholder, Charles Thysell, and Jack Youngquist. According to a recent Rourke Art Gallery and Museum newsletter, the gallery holds over five thousand regional artworks in its permanent collection.

After Jim O'Rourke died, I went to the estate sale with a friend, and I was able to see his home. To sum up my impressions, it was cluttered! I saw more antiques and collectibles than paintings during my visit. Perhaps the art from his collections had already been moved to the Rourke Gallery?

The community of Fargo-Moorhead saluted Jim O'Rourke when he died in 2011 with newspaper tributes and more. Some of the descriptions his colleagues utilized to describe him included:

- *A life devoted to art*
- *A proud man, but a difficult man*
- *He was wildly passionate and enigmatic*
- *His way was the right way*
- *He's the only person who could have inspired art in the middle of the frozen tundra*
- *He was the driver of the bus. Come on board, but Jim O'Rourke would determine where the bus was going*
- *Autocratic, irascible, and difficult to work with*
- *His intensity was formidable*

Others described him as: "A brilliant collector of important art and a builder of the arts community. His dedication to the visual arts was legendary. Both his public and personal art collections are world class."

The Rourke Gallery, Plains Art Museum, and the Red River Arts Center were all located in the historic

Moorhead post office building in 1966, but by 1975, the Plains and the Red River Arts Center had moved to different locations. Jack remained on the boards of both the Rourke Gallery and the Plains Art Museum. In 1997, the Plains Art Museum began a campaign to purchase a building in Fargo, but Jack was already gone. Today, The Rourke Gallery is the only art organization occupying the old post office in Moorhead.

Jack was a founding board member of the Rourke Gallery in 1973, and of the Plains Art Museum in 1975, according to a handwritten note by Jim O'Rourke to Jack's parents following Jack's death in 1986. Jack's mother, Dorothy, sent me a copy of O'Rourke's note after Jack's funeral. The note also said that a woodcut by Charles Beck was given to the Rourke Gallery and became a part of the gallery's permanent collection as a memorial to Jack.[28]

14. Forensics, Then and Now

North Dakota Cold Cases

THE YEAR MY FRIEND JACK was murdered, there were ten homicides in North Dakota. North Dakota's total population in 1986 was 679,000. Currently, North Dakota has a murder clearance rate of 90 percent, which means that nine out of ten murders are solved on average.

The unsolved cases have been my focus for this book because I had a friend whose murder has been unsolved for thirty-five years. If your family member or friend was the one murder that had remained unsolved, you would know how I feel.

North Dakota Attorney General Wayne Stenehjem established a cold case program in November 2005. Today, there are twelve unsolved North Dakota murders, along with seven cold cases for missing persons. The attorney general added to his announcement regarding the new cold case initiative, "There is no statute of limitations for homicide cases, so with sufficient evidence, a prosecution can take place at any time, as long as the perpetrator is still alive." The attorney general also noted that, over time, relationships change. For example, a family death or divorce might provide the impetus to share information, especially if that family member was a threat in some way. Sometimes new investigators bring "fresh eyes" to the case.

Another reason for establishing a cold case initiative is that, as time goes by, new discovery techniques are developed. For example, DNA analysis became widely accepted by 2001, but DNA was not a tool for law enforcement in 1986; no samples were saved from the autopsy for DNA analysis in Jack's murder.

The unsolved Wahl murder was not included in the initial group of unsolved murders when the cold case squad was announced in 2005. Instead, the Wahl case is still considered an "open and inactive" case.

Improving the System

Today, fewer than 10 percent of the police departments in the US have units dedicated to cold cases. Most states and cities cite a lack of funding for cold cases, since priorities usually focus on current investigations. One contemporary trend is for law enforcement agencies to hire recently retired officers and detectives to focus on cold cases, but this also takes funding.

The New York City Police Department recently announced that, prior to the COVID pandemic, they had a 90 percent clearance rate for murders.[29] The clearance rate dropped to 60 percent in 2020. There were simply other priorities, and of course a reduced police workforce added to that problem. It will take time to return to a 90 percent clearance rate.

A helpful new tool is the use of surveillance cameras for homes and businesses, as well as police cameras worn by officers. Both DNA technology and surveillance tapes can be shared with other law enforcement agencies to help solve murder investigations today, but in most cases, sharing that information with other states requires changes in state laws.

Recently, Nebraska passed legislation that compels people to submit to a DNA swab after they have been convicted of a felony. The sample is submitted to a national database used to explore whether the felon is linked to other crimes. The Nebraska legislature enhanced this in 2021 by approving a bill that would allow police to collect DNA samples from people who are charged with but not yet convicted of violent crimes.[30]

Alaska is one of thirty-one states requiring DNA samples upon arrest or when criminal charges have been filed. These samples would be added to the FBI'S CODIS database. Since 1995, 21,577 arrests have been made where no DNA sample was completed as required, either because officers weren't well-trained or they simply ignored the requirement.

Since the newest Alaska law was passed in 2007, 1,555 of the criminals in this group have died. The Alaska attorney general has ordered that the remaining 20,000 criminals who are still living must contribute to the DNA database. Recently, the state of Alaska has sent letters to each of the criminals to comply or face contempt charges.

In May 2021, US Congressmen Michael McCaul of Texas and Eric Swalwell of California, introduced a bipartisan bill known as the *Homicide Victims' Families Rights Act* to provide expanded rights to the families of homicide victims in federal cases. Both congressmen are former prosecutors, and thus attorneys. The House bill (H.R.3359) was referred to the US Subcommittee on Crime, Terrorism, and Homeland Security on November 9, 2021.[31] There are now thirteen co-sponsors (twelve Democrats, one Republican). North Dakota's lone congressman, Kelly Armstrong, is not a co-sponsor.

US Representative McCaul utilized the true story of a thirty-year-old brutal murder of four young girls in his news release, stating, "To this day, we do not know who is responsible. The families and others like them should be able to work with law enforcement to pursue justice on behalf of their loved ones." US Representative Swalwell added, "Accountability is crucial to begin the healing process." The proposed bill lists the following as homicide survivors: spouses, children, partners, siblings, and friends.

The congressmen recommend that if a case has gone cold after *three* years, relatives should have the right to have their family member's case reviewed and loved ones should be notified when there are updates on the case. The proposal would also collect data regarding the problems encountered in each cold case to improve the system.

The Murder Accountability Project, utilizing FBI data, sponsored by McCaul and Swalwell, highlights the growing number of unsolved cases: "The percentage of homicides where someone has been charged has declined from 95 percent in 1965 to 65 percent in 2018.

Since 1980, when these records began, over 250,000 American citizens have been murdered, and no one has been charged."

Technological Advances

Technology in 1986 was not at all like the technology we take for granted today. In 1986, my family was fortunate to have a Betamax system to record television shows. This home video system was developed for use in 1984, so the technology was very new. I remember that the Salaba's had a laser disc system that looked like a seventy-eight record and played popular movies. Jack, however, had the latest video system in his lower-level family room, a projection TV system. I don't know of any other homes that had one at the time.

The video projector is just how it sounds. An image is projected onto a large screen with three light bulbs— red, blue, and green to mix the color images. (This was also called a *CRT projector* for the cathode ray tube utilized to generate the images.) By 2000, the CRT projector was replaced with LCD projectors.

The movie that the housekeeper found playing on Jack's big-screen TV was *Deep Throat*, one of the first pornographic movies on video tape designed for in-home use. *Deep Throat* was released in 1972 and starred Linda Lovelace. It soon became a cult classic. The movie features seventeen explicit sex scenes. Although it is still thought of as a classic for those famous sex scenes, I don't remember it as having a gay theme. Instead, *Deep Throat* is remembered as one of the first movies with a "sex theme" from the "golden age" of pornography (1969-1984). Home viewing made it popular, since it was rated "R."

When the investigation began, Dr. Watkin asked whether there was a movie playing on the VCR. Agent Latozke added, "Yes, and the movie was *Deep Throat*." Dr. Jensen, who was the first doctor on the scene, verified that there was noise coming from the TV and that he asked the EMTs to turn down the sound so that he could check Jack's vital signs. And it was the noise coming from the basement that Betty Hanson noticed when she arrived at Jack's house that Thursday morning. She was surprised to hear anything coming from the lower level. The door to the basement was ajar, too, which was unusual. As she entered the family room downstairs, she heard the movie playing.

Communications Technology

New technology—including the World Wide Web (WWW), cell phones, and social media—have made communications around the world far-reaching and instantaneous. It is difficult to remember the world of fax machines and land lines that existed at the time of this murder. Communications still relied on telephone and "snail" mail through the US postal system.

There were no cell phones in 1986. Mobile phones were developed in the 1980s, but most wireless telephones were installed in cars or work vehicles at the time of the murder, and I didn't know anyone who had one. Cell phones became more common in the late 1990s, but by today's standards, they were huge, heavy, difficult to carry, and not very useful.

There was no emergency 9-1-1 system in 1986, either. The 1985 North Dakota Legislature had approved a tax of fifty cents per household to implement a 9-1-1 system, but there was no 9-1-1 system in place in Pembina County in 1986. Nationally, the 9-1-1 system was established in 1968, but it wasn't in place across the state of North Dakota until 2005.

If you had lived in a rural area during this time, you would remember that each of the rural roads had to be numbered before the 9-1-1 system could work. After the roads were numbered for the first time, rural residents had a "street" address, so emergency services could find all the rural homes rather than relying on landmarks. It would take several more years before Pembina County was included in the GPS (Global Positioning System) which utilized satellites to pinpoint a location.

Information moved more slowly in 1986. The internet as we know it today was developed in 1969, and email technology was launched in 1972; however, the World Wide Web wasn't really utilized in a broad way until 1989, and nothing else like it was used by a wide cross section of people in the '80s. When I was working in Cavalier, we were just happy to have fax machines.

Investigation Technology

It's hard to remember a time before surveillance cameras were everywhere, as well. In 1986, no one had security systems at home, and police officers didn't wear body cameras. Technology has changed how crimes are studied today. AFIS, the national automated fingerprint identification system, was still in its infancy in the 1980s. Today, we have both facial recognition and fingerprint identification on our own individual cellular phones!

A new and controversial surveillance system, known as *Google Geofence*, was first utilized in 2018, and privacy rights advocates don't like it. While most search warrants require "probable cause," Geofence can pinpoint everyone who carried a cell phone in the vicinity of a crime and search their data through their phone, their Facebook account, or email address. Some legal authorities stress that this type of search might be unconstitutional, although it hasn't been tested in the courts yet. The Fourth Amendment protects US citizens from "illegal search and seizure." In 2020, Geofence warrants were requested 11,554 times—so stay tuned!

Social media is so extensive today that law enforcement regularly uses these platforms to release information to the general public in their search for evidence. More recently, social media platforms are being utilized to solve cold cases, making it more efficient for investigators to gather information. Still, only 20 percent of cold cases are ever solved.

DNA

My understanding is that stab wounds result in a lot of blood loss. There would be blood splatter too. Today, investigators would conduct a blood pattern or blood splatter analysis, which would help to identify the direction of the blow, the type of weapon, the severity of the injury, and evidence of a struggle.

DNA technology was not available in 1986 when my friend Jack was murdered. I remember asking Sonny Dump, the BCI investigator, years later about the possibility of DNA. I was told that since DNA wasn't commonly used in 1986, no samples were saved from the Wahl murder investigation for this purpose. DNA, or deoxyribonucleic acid, is the "molecular blueprint" for humans. DNA profiling to solve crimes began in 1985 in England. Every individual has a unique combination of cells with links to their relatives. Sources of DNA evidence may include saliva from cigarette butts, bottles, and drink glasses. Forensic scientists often gather these small bits of evidence from a crime scene wearing gloves and other protection, so as not to contaminate the crime scene. (I don't know if the Pembina County investigators wore gloves or if it was a standard procedure at that time.)

There are four classes of DNA: private, research, public opt-in, and public opt-out. A recent development in DNA research revolves around privacy. Today, law enforcement agencies of all sizes regularly utilize DNA to solve crimes. In fact, DNA has been very effective at solving years-old crimes that have gone cold. In 2018, Joseph James DeAngelo, known as the "Golden State Killer," was apprehended using DNA and genealogical research to solve a cold case.

Initially, DNA was utilized to establish paternity. The first criminal conviction using DNA in the US was in 1987. By 2001, DNA was generally accepted as dependable evidence. Today, DNA and a new tool, *genetic genealogy*, are commonly utilized to solve cold cases.

A conventional DNA profile includes twenty markers. Everyone has a unique DNA profile, like a fingerprint. Basically, people leave behind trace amounts of hair, saliva, blood, semen, sweat, skin cells, or mucus wherever they go.

Forensic investigators are now utilizing familial DNA searches as a last resort because of legal and privacy issues. Familial DNA is not exact, but it reduces the number of suspects. It has been utilized in unsolved homicides where investigators have exhausted all other leads. Sometimes family members voluntarily contribute DNA to cold cases to help find missing persons, or to help the police identify a body. Today, many missing-persons cases are solved by simply retrieving a molar from an unidentified homicide victim to test for DNA. In forensic investigations, a lot has changed in thirty-five years.

One of the primary DNA issues revolves around the privacy of commercial databases. Two common consumer DNA tests are performed through 23andMe.com and Ancestry.com. These tests are utilized by consumers to track their family genetics. The problem with law enforcement accessing this private DNA testing is that the owner has not given permission for it to be used this way. Another problem is that everyone a person is related to may be included in a commercial search, and they haven't given permission at all.

GED Match and Family Tree DNA are two of the companies that collect voluntary DNA uploads by individuals.[32] In 2019, both companies changed their policies to allow an "opt-in" for law enforcement searches. Neither Ancestry.com nor 23andMe.com allows collected data to be shared with law enforcement at this time. GED Match was recently sold because it couldn't manage the privacy issues. The newly combined company, known as Verogen, will now sell its services to law enforcement agencies with an addendum: any identifying information supplied to police must be corroborated by other means.[33]

Differences among the States

Five states have laws and policies regarding familial DNA searches (California, Florida, New York, Wisconsin, and Colorado) and one state has laws forbidding a familial search (Maryland). Sometimes, family DNA results in a partial match and more approvals are needed.

One of the most memorable cases tied to DNA is the 1996 death of JonBenét Ramsay in Colorado. Her parents were eventually exonerated in 2008 as the result of DNA testing, although the case is still unsolved, and both parents have died. (Note: There are still one thousand three hundred active cold cases in this state as of January 2021, according to *Out There Colorado*.)[34]

Massachusetts State Senator Ann Gobi and State Representative Todd Smola have submitted a bill called *Act Permitting Familial Searching and Partial DNA Matches in Investigating Certain Unsolved Cases* (S.1595). Senator Gobi explains, "If we can solve some of these old crimes . . . if there are still killers walking around, let's get them." The family of Molly Bish added, "When you've spent twenty years in a club that no one wants to belong to, you get really close to other victim's families." Massachusetts already has a law mandating taking a DNA sample from anyone convicted of a crime.[35]

Molly Bish was sixteen when she disappeared in Massachusetts in 2000. Her sister, Heather Bish, meets yearly with investigators for updates on the twenty-year-old homicide, and sees the potential uses of partial DNA and an emerging technology called *DNA Phenotyping*, especially when the only evidence available includes old samples, skeletal remains, or contaminated evidence. A Texas-based company, Othram, Inc., is now specializing in finding DNA markers in older and/or partial or degraded evidence.

Phenotyping is a technique where a person's physical profile is reverse engineered. The company most known for this discovery is called Parabon NanoLabs. The technique has not been peer-reviewed, and as a result, at this writing it is sometimes discredited. Parabon is reluctant to publicize their findings in peer-reviewed journals because the company is worried about disclosing its trade secrets.

Another dimension of DNA research has had a different result. Since 1989, over one hundred fifty people have been released from prison utilizing DNA science as a result of the Innocence Project. Innocence Project, Inc. was established in 1992 by two lawyers who served on the legal team for the O.J. Simpson trial. The goal of this non-profit organization is "to exonerate the wrongly convicted through DNA testing."

Today, the FBI maintains a database known as CODIS,[36] with DNA profiles collected by local, state, and federal law enforcement officers. All fifty states now maintain DNA databases. In 1994, uniform standards for data collection were developed for CODIS. It is now common to issue "John Doe" warrants when DNA has been collected, but a match has not surfaced (yet) through CODIS. Once evidence is entered into CODIS, it will always remain in the system, whether there is a solution to a case or not.

Types of Murder Cases

The Wahl murder investigation has been an *open* or *inactive* file for more than thirty-five years. It has never been cleared. New technology along with social media has helped to shed light on some cold cases, but not this one. Today, this small-town murder investigation is still an open case, but it is not considered a *cold* case by the North Dakota attorney general's office. A cold case is defined as "an unsolved criminal investigation that is no longer being actively pursued due to lack of evidence."

According to an interview with the University of Western Ontario's Michael Arntfield, a criminology professor, "Cleared cases are files that have an official resolution, either by way of criminal charges or some other form of closure."[37] The Wahl murder case is in limbo.

Sometimes the case is closed because the primary suspect has died and is unable to defend him/herself in court. Pembina County Sheriff Glenn Wells and State's

Attorney Robert Lee released a six-point statement that was reported in the *Grand Forks Herald* on December 13, 1986.[38] One of the points included "Evidence at this time indicates the person who last saw Dr. Wahl alive is dead." District Judge James O'Keefe refused to call a grand jury based on this statement. The Pembina County authorities believe that John Nelson murdered Jack Wahl.

In most states, first-degree murder is defined as an unlawful killing that is both *willful* and *premeditated*. This means that the crime was committed after planning or "lying in wait for the victim." In some states, willfulness must also be shown. This is defined as specific intent to end a human life. In addition, some states include *malice* as part of the definition for first-degree murder, i.e., "an evil disposition or purpose and an indifference to human life."

Second-degree murder is generally defined as intentional murder that lacks premeditation. The act is intended to cause bodily harm, although the murderer disregards the possibility that the act will kill someone.

Manslaughter is defined as an unlawful killing that doesn't involve malice or intent to hurt or kill, but someone has died as the result of a reckless disregard for life.[39] There are two categories: (1) involuntary and (2) voluntary. The difference between the two types of manslaughter is based on whether the death resulted from extreme recklessness or negligence and whether a felony was also involved.

No one has ever been charged in my friend Jack's murder, and there is no current activity on the case with the exception of my current research.

15. Means, Motive, and Opportunity

H AVE YOU EVER HAD A friend or family member die suddenly? If you have had this experience, you probably know how it feels when you aren't able to say goodbye. When the sudden death isn't due to an illness or a car accident, but instead an unsolved murder, it's a wound that just doesn't heal, because the unanswered questions are haunting. The only thing worse is not locating the body. Open cases also lead, especially in a small town where everybody knows each other, to making everyone seem suspicious.

When a murder investigation begins, three factors are considered: (1) who had the *means* to commit murder; (2) who had a good *motive* to murder; and (3) who had an *opportunity* to carry it out.

The means includes a murder weapon. In the case of this unsolved murder, the local investigators knew that the murderer used a knife of some kind. The weapon was never recovered or even sufficiently identified. The local investigators never publicly revealed a motive for the murder, but they implied that it was due to Jack's lifestyle.

According to the autopsy, and as reported in the *Grand Forks Herald*,[40] Jack had been stabbed six times in the chest, back, and side. There were no signs of a struggle or forced entry, so this indicates that the murderer was probably someone who was invited into Jack's home and/or who knew him.

Hunches, and a Review of the Past

Jack's unsolved murder impacted my life along with the lives of many others, including his family, of course. I hope that writing this book will help to raise awareness about the many murder investigations that reach a "dead end," take years to solve, or go "cold," leaving friends and family wondering *what* happened, and *why*. I encourage readers to carry their hunches to whoever might be able to act on the information they have either stumbled across or pieced together, in the hope that someone will listen. This is exactly what I did in 2020. I began by reviewing what is known of the case.

The final report, released by Sheriff Glenn Wells just before his retirement in December 1986, states that nothing was missing from the house, and that the prime suspect was now dead. Glenn Wells was convinced that twenty-three-year-old John Nelson committed the murder. I am not.

I have conceived of a possible suspect who had means, a motive, and opportunity. My suspect was also known for his temper. The Cavalier area investigators wouldn't have known him. And since I was never interviewed by law enforcement, even if I'd thought of this person as a suspect in 1986, I wouldn't have had an opportunity to share it with the investigators. It took years of speculation and several coincidences before I arrived at this theory of the crime.

A North Dakota Bureau of Criminal Investigations (BCI) agent named Sonny Dump was asked to join the murder investigation by Pembina County State's Attorney Bob Lee and the sheriff's department. (The BCI is also known as the State Police.) The BCI is usually invited into the investigation by the local state's attorney, especially when the investigation is at a standstill. According to the investigation notes acquired through the open records (FOIA) request earlier this year (July 2021), Deputy Sheriff Joe Martindale contacted Sonny Dump within an hour of surveying the crime scene on February 13, 1986.

As part of the investigation, Investigator Dump developed a *victimology* study of the background, education, mannerisms, and lifestyle of the victim. Such reports may also touch on the relationships of the offender to the victim. The BCI investigator explained in a newspaper interview in the *Grand Forks Herald*[41] that this information usually reveals a profile of the murderer that is usually 85-95 percent accurate.

The initial call for ambulance service was received at 8:44 a.m. Doctors Jensen, Larson, Watkin, and Tareen arrived at Jack's house prior to the law enforcement contingent. When the Pembina County deputy sheriff arrived, he told everyone to leave, including Betty Hanson, who had placed the call for an ambulance. Joe Martindale then contacted Cavalier Police Chief John Reynolds to secure the entrance to Jack's house.

A $5,000 reward for any information regarding the Wahl murder was widely communicated. Later, the Wahl family increased the reward to $10,000, but it didn't help to solve the case. Thirty-five years later, as I write this story, the reward has not been distributed and the investigation is inactive—but not cold and not closed.

The Pembina County sheriff and other community members in Cavalier seemed to think that there was a gay motive in the murder from the beginning. Several of my friends were questioned following the murder, including my brother-in-law, Mark Gregory, and friends including Kenny Askew and Jim Salaba. Today, Kenny is living as openly gay in Minneapolis, and Jim Salaba has moved to the state of Washington, where he has a long-term relationship with another man. Both men stated in their interviews that Jack had never approached them sexually.

Mark married his longtime girlfriend, Barb, in 2006. Mark and Barb had dated until they started college. Mark went to UND in Grand Forks, and she enrolled in nearby NDSU in Fargo. Barb married someone she met in college, moved to a small town in the middle of North Dakota, and had two sons. She divorced her husband in the early 1980s and enrolled in graduate school at UND as a single mom. Barb went on to complete a doctoral degree in psychology. Eventually, she married Mark after a long engagement. They built a house across the street from Oliver Gregory's home in Cavalier.

A young, local guy, John Nelson, killed himself after being questioned in the murder investigation. To this day, many people in Cavalier think that John Nelson killed Jack. This theory was reinforced by Sheriff Wells and Judge O'Keefe through newspaper reports. Both men reported that the person responsible for the murder was now dead. In fact, Judge O'Keefe gave this as the reason he wouldn't call a grand jury. The investigators didn't openly say that there was a gay angle to the murder, but implied that Jack's lifestyle put him in jeopardy.

Who Done It?

I have had thirty-five years to think about *who* would want to kill my friend Jack. *Why* would someone want to end Jack's life? *How* did law enforcement members come to a conclusion that nothing was stolen, and that robbery was not the motive? *What* was the killer's motivation? I don't believe it was a stranger who killed my friend. I believe it was someone who knew Jack and was angry with him.

Let's start by discussing the two people Jack was with during his last night on earth. First, there was Jim Salaba. Jim and Jack had dinner with a local widow named Jean Speckman on Wednesday, February 12, 1986, at the Cedar Inn. All three individuals had been friends for more than ten years. People have speculated that both men were gay. If they were, I don't believe that they had any type of sexual relationship. (It would have been too difficult in a small town to pull that off.)

I spent a lot of time with both Jack and Jim and I also traveled with them. I have also had several gay friends during my lifetime. I would have known if there was an attraction. My observation was that both well-educated men were lonely and were simply good friends who enjoyed each other's company.

Back to the possible suspects: Kenny, our gardener, had some classic gay characteristics as a kid. He came out of the "closet" after college. I don't think that Jack would have pursued a gay relationship with a boy living in a small town, and on the other hand, I don't believe Jack would have put himself in a position to have a relationship with a child, ethically. He also would have too much to lose. Kenny was, and still is, so mild-mannered that it is difficult to see him fighting off a gay advance, and then stabbing the attacker. I will rule out Kenny as a suspect in the murder, even if my friend Jack lived a secret life.

The next two possible suspects I have mentioned were adults who interacted frequently with Jack, primarily through work. Both Neil Fleming and David Watkin were highly educated, married with children, and very controlling. They didn't appreciate Jack as a person, but instead saw him as a competitor. And since Jack was very popular in the community with people of all ages, and since the other men were neither friendly nor popular, their interactions with Jack would often lead to conflict. Jack tolerated both men but didn't consider them friends and would never socialize with them.

At the time of the murder there was some antagonism between Jack and Neil Fleming over the assisted living complex the hospital board members were planning to build near the nursing home. Neil's cousin, an architect, had designed the nursing home building, and Neil wanted to involve him again in the new building. As president of the hospital board, Neil wanted to control the project.

Jack was the physician's representative to the hospital board and shared the opinion that the nursing home was poorly designed. He wanted a different architect for the apartment building, though. This argument had been going on for over a year and would be well documented in the hospital board minutes. I don't believe that Neil Fleming could have stabbed anyone to death, but he had been trained to kill as an Army officer during the Vietnam era.

Dr. David Watkin was the other local person who had conflict with Jack at the time of the murder. Dr. Watkin felt that Jack was complicit in getting Mark out of harm's way when he crashed a car while having a medical incident. I would describe Watkin's demeanor as righteous. He thought Jack was covering for Mark and wanted to make sure that Jack knew that Dr. Watkin had his own power and could make trouble for Jack.

Dr. Watkin threatened to describe the situation to the medical licensing board, which would put Jack in jeopardy if there were any basis to Dr. Watkin's assumptions. There was no love lost between the two physicians, but I can't believe that the animosity would escalate to the point of murder.

I was surprised at how Dr. Watkin interjected his opinions when the murder investigation began on February 13, 1986. According to the investigation notes, he focused on Jack's coat or jacket, then the fact that there were three beers on the coffee table. Watkin then offered, "The thing that's going to make it real hard is Jack, over the years, had a lot of late-night visitors, people would come at ungodly hours." Watkin also questioned the tape playing on the VCR. In my review of the notes, it seems like Dave Watkin was targeting specific evidence in his conversations with the investigators—while never mentioning that he and Jack had been fighting the previous week.

Since I knew that Dave Watkin was never invited to Jack's social events, I was surprised that Watkin positioned himself as an authority on Jack's social life. In addition, Dr. Watkin lived in another part of town, so it was odd that he focused on the late-night visitors. He wouldn't have been able to observe visitors at Wahl's house, like Dr. Tareen could, living next door to Jack.

I suppose the murderer could have been a stranger to me or the community, someone passing through town, or someone who had met Jack previously and knew where he lived. The police report indicates a tennis shoe print on the passenger side of Jack's car, which was parked in the garage. None of the witnesses who saw Jack during the last night of his life indicated that anyone accompanied Jack to his home when he left Stu's Pub. As I never saw Jack wearing tennis shoes himself, I think the shoe imprint likely was from the newspaper delivery boy, who always left the paper in the garage. Shouldn't the investigators have followed up on the tennis shoe print in the garage and identified the newspaper deliverer? I didn't see anything in the investigation notes referencing these clues at all.

As a suspect, I believe John Nelson, age twenty-three, was simply in the wrong place at the wrong time. He was among the last to see Jack alive, and maybe he witnessed something or saw someone at Jack's house. In the suicide letter to his parents, John implied that he had contemplated suicide previously. I believe that he was simply fragile, had low self-esteem, and felt powerless when questioned by law enforcement. He simply decided to take himself out rather than try to defend himself. It was easier.

The Murder Weapon

The investigation notes make it plain that some type of knife was used to kill Jack, but the notes are sparse when it comes to how the investigators pursued this piece of evidence.

It would have been relatively easy to toss a knife in rural Pembina County somewhere on the way to Manitoba, Canada, or to Grand Forks and beyond. It would never be found in a snow-filled ditch in February, and there are a lot of ditches in Pembina County. Where would you begin to look for a discarded weapon? It would be remarkable to find a Chicago Cutlery knife in a ditch in the spring, but who would be looking for it? I mention that brand of knife because that's the only question Sheriff Glenn Wells asked me in September 1986.

16. I Follow Up

Following Up

O N OCTOBER 26, 2003, I drafted a letter to the Pembina County sheriff, outlining some information that I had discovered while living in Fargo, North Dakota. I also asked if computer technology or DNA research could help to resolve the still unsolved 1986 murder in Cavalier. I had wanted to share my thoughts and ideas about the investigation too, but I never heard back from the Pembina County group.

By 2004, each of the law enforcement officials had changed in Pembina County, either through retirement or death, and both Dr. Warren Jensen and Pembina County State's Attorney Bob Lee had moved out of town. Dr. Jensen was living in Grand Forks, North Dakota. Bob Lee initially moved to Fargo but was now retired and living in Washington State.

Freedom of Information

Under North Dakota's open records laws,[42] law enforcement records are archived in three different categories: (1) confidential; (2) exempt or discretionary; and

(3) open. Discretionary records are not confidential. They *can* be released to the public if law enforcement officials or the local state's attorney cooperates. Eventually, a murder case or investigation will be classified as either: open, closed, active, or inactive.

In North Dakota, anyone has the right to inspect any record held by any public agency, unless purposely exempted by law. Any agency that receives public funding is required to share information through this public records law. There is no statute of limitations on a murder investigation in North Dakota, however statutes change over time.[43] There is always the possibility that new evidence will surface and make the case active again.

North Dakota Freedom of Information Act (FOIA), or open records law (NDCC 44-04-18),[44] includes paper documents, email, photography, or audio/video files. Active criminal *intelligence* information and active criminal *investigative* information are not subject to NDCC 44-04-18 (North Dakota Century Code).

In general, open case files in North Dakota can be requested by the general public when the case has been closed. When there is no longer any activity on the case, and there will be no further investigation activities, the files are considered public information.

Anyone has the right to review or get a copy of the public records, regardless of the reason for the request or where they live. The public entity cannot ask why the records are being requested. If the request is denied, the public entity must explain what specific federal or state law makes the public record closed or inaccessible. I filed an open records request with the current

Pembina County state's attorney on October 12, 2020. They agreed to sharing files and meeting with me. The state's attorney referred me to the sheriff.

I met with Pembina County Sheriff Terry Meidinger at his office. Deputy Sheriff Marcus Ramsay also participated in this meeting. I had previously filed a Freedom of Information Act request in October 2020, which included a list of items I asked to see. The officials had received permission from the current state's attorney to share the information. The investigation notes were typed by a secretary in the sheriff's office from the handwritten notes the investigators had accumulated. (The notes were typed in 1986, and there were no computer files.) None of the photography, video, or audio files were requested for my research, but they probably would have had to be transferred to new technology to view them anyway. The deputy photocopied the written files for me. Technology has changed a lot since 1986!

In 1997, the region experienced the biggest flood event ever recorded. As a result, many of the files from the *Grand Forks Herald* were destroyed by water and a major fire. It was a lucky break for me that I had kept each of the newspaper reports on the investigation from 1986, and that I was interested in following up on this case, or the investigation would continue to age on the law enforcement shelves forever.

In 2004, North Dakota Attorney General Stenehjem provided an opinion on inactive cases for clarification for law enforcement:

A case is not active when the county state's attorney does not intend to move forward on the matter and no

one knows if the suspect will ever return to this coun-
try. There must be a reasonable, good faith anticipation
of securing an arrest or prosecution in the foreseeable
future. If the case is not "active," the criminal investiga-
tive information is open to the public (N.D.A.G. 2004-
0-03, January 20, 2004).

All of the law enforcement officials originally involved in the Wahl murder case are dead, including Sheriff Glenn Wells, Pembina County Deputy Sheriff Joe Martindale, and North Dakota Bureau of Criminal Investigations Agent Detective Sonny Dump. There are new people in the law enforcement departments now, including the Pembina County state's attorney—who are not familiar with the case, and most of them are too young to remember it or have moved to Cavalier from another region.

Crime Statistics

I also conducted research into broader areas of crime. According to Pew Research, "Most violent and property crimes in the US go unsolved."[45] Here are some of the findings from the Pew Research report:

- FBI statistics reflect the percentage of crimes cleared through arrest or "exceptional means," including cases where the suspect dies or the victim doesn't cooperate with a prosecution.
- Most of the reported crimes don't result in the arrest, charging, and prosecution of a suspect.

- In 2015, only 47 percent of the violent crimes tracked by the Bureau of Justice Statistics (BJS) were reported to the police.
- There is a significant variation in reporting and solving crimes depending on the offense.
- 61.5 percent of the murders cleared by police in 2015 included non-negligent manslaughter.[46]

According to another contributor to the Pew Research report:[47]
- In 1972, the US Supreme Court issued a moratorium on the death penalty.
- In 1996, 78 percent of US adults *favored* the death penalty for persons convicted of murder; in 2018, only 54 percent were in favor.[48]
- In 1996, 18 percent of the population *opposed* the death penalty for persons convicted of murder; in 2018, 39 percent were opposed to the death penalty for persons convicted of murder.
- Public support for the death penalty reached a four-decade low in 2016 but has increased somewhat since then.
- Support for the death penalty has long been divided by gender and race. Most men favor the death penalty (61 percent) while only 46 percent of the women surveyed favored the death penalty.
- The 2015 study of attitudes toward capital punishment, found that 63 percent of

the public thought the death penalty was morally justified but worried that there is some risk of an innocent person being put to death (71 percent); most people surveyed didn't believe that the death penalty deterred serious crime (61 percent).

When Cold Cases Are Revisited

North Dakota Attorney General Wayne Stenehjem launched a Cold Case Investigations initiative in November 2005. In a news release announcing that program, Stenehjem stated, "Someone may be keeping a terrible secret. As unsolved cases grow colder, a murderer may be growing more confident that the secret is safe, but victims and their families are entitled to know that law enforcement never rests. There is no statute of limitations for a homicide case, so with sufficient evidence a prosecution can take place at any time *as long as the perpetrator is still alive.*" Stenehjem also said, "Cold Case Investigations will utilize advances in forensics and DNA technology along with new investigative techniques to review evidence and explore new leads." Such investigators reexamine police files, autopsy records, and evidence, and they may reinterview witnesses to try and solve a cold case.

Cold cases are being reviewed around the country. Lycoming, Pennsylvania, cold case detective Kenneth L. Mains has stated, "Sometimes a detective doesn't contribute to a cold case by solving it, but instead by moving it forward with a fresh set of eyes." He further explained, "Cold cases are most likely to be reopened under the following circumstances"[49] (in ranked order):

1. New witness information
2. Availability of DNA to submit to databases
3. New information from citizens or informants
4. IAFIS—quality fingerprint evidence
5. Availability of outstanding leads
6. Murder weapon recovered
7. Suspect identified
8. Recovery of projectiles or casings to submit to databases
9. Potential of obtaining additional witness information
10. Case fits serial pattern
11. Victim identified
12. Evidence properly handled and stored
13. Case file complete and retrievable
14. Aggravating circumstances (innocence of victim, hate crime, heinousness of crime)
15. Original investigator case notes available
16. Queries from family members
17. Original investigator available for interview
18. Statute of limitations about to expire
19. Media attention paid to case

Tampa, Florida, currently has two hundred forty murder cases that are classified as "cold." On August 6, 2021, Hillsborough Law Enforcement, which includes

Tampa, announced that two investigators have recently been hired for a Cold Case Unit, in an attempt to solve some of these old cold cases. The county has also launched a podcast on unsolved murders, called "Unfinished Business," to enlist the help of the general public. This is a unique, new way to utilize technology to help to solve murder investigations.

Other jurisdictions are also using podcasts to try to close cases. One locale features unsolved crimes during the month they occurred. Another community uses podcasts to feature unsolved murders every month. Usually, rewards are featured along with anonymous reporting systems. Since this use of technology targets the general public, it may have more success.

However, there is no universal definition of a cold case in the United States. Some jurisdictions consider that a case has gone cold when all of the investigation leads have been exhausted. Others consider the length of time that has elapsed since the crime occurred.

The National Institute of Justice defines a cold case as:

A case such as a violent crime, missing person, or unidentified person that has remained unsolved for at least three years and has the potential to be solved through newly acquired information or advanced technology.

As you might expect, murder cases can be "chilled" for a variety of reasons, including lack of leads, fading memories, loss of evidence, and the fact that new cases are prioritized.

Sharing Clues

So many things had changed since 1986, including DNA testing, social media, and new technology. I felt that I had enough clues to contact both the North Dakota US Attorney and the North Dakota Attorney General again. I knew both gentlemen from my community activities and felt comfortable sharing my ideas about my friend Jack's untimely death.

US Attorney for North Dakota Drew Wrigley responded to my email inquiry in 2004. He reported speaking with Sonny Dump, the BCI investigator, about Jack's murder. Drew encouraged me to talk with Wayne Stenehjem, North Dakota's attorney general, and told me that it didn't sound like DNA evidence was collected as part of the Wahl investigation. He went on to explain the jurisdiction he had and told me that the (new) Pembina County state's attorney still had jurisdiction over the 1986 murder investigation.

Both Drew Wrigley and Wayne Stenehjem are still serving as North Dakota's US attorney and attorney general at this writing. In 2018, Drew Wrigley was again appointed US attorney, this time by President Donald Trump.[50] In the interim, he served as North Dakota Lieutenant Governor under Governor Jack Dalrymple, and had been Chief of Staff under Governor John Hoeven, who is now a US senator.

Wayne Stenehjem had served in the North Dakota Legislature for more than twenty years prior to running for the state's attorney general position and winning in 2000. Each year, the North Dakota Office of

Attorney General submits a special report regarding homicides in the state, defined as:

> *The willful killing of one human being by another. It does not include attempts to kill, assaults to kill, suicides, accidental deaths, justifiable homicides, or deaths caused by gross negligence.*

The *Forum*, North Dakota's largest newspaper, reported thirty-two homicides in North Dakota during 2020, the highest number since records began in 1978. This compares to twenty-six homicides in 2019. According to the Attorney General, North Dakota had 4.2 homicides per 100,000 population which compares to 5.0/100,000 in the US (in 2020). The number of homicides has increased in North Dakota since the oil boom began in 2006. The population has also increased to 765,309 during this time.

Homicide statistics for North Dakota indicate that 69 percent of the crimes were committed by males, and that 12/32 were homicides related to domestic relationships. Eighty-eight percent of the homicides were cleared (28/32) in 2020.[51]

A Case in Point

A more recent case demonstrating that the murderer gets better treatment—and more chances—than the victim comes from 2003. Drew Wrigley had been appointed US Attorney for North Dakota by President George W. Bush in 2001 and served until 2009. During this time he tried a murder case that ended in a federal death penalty conviction in September 2006. The US attorney's office was the lead on the 2003 murder case because it crossed state lines.

North Dakota abolished its death penalty in 1973 and does not have a current death penalty statute, but since the case crossed state borders, the federal death penalty was in play. It was the first death penalty case in North Dakota in a century.

A UND college student from Minnesota, Dru Sjodin (age twenty-two), was kidnapped at a North Dakota shopping center in Grand Forks, North Dakota, in November 2003, and murdered in nearby Minnesota. (Grand Forks is located on the North Dakota-Minnesota border.) Her body was found in a ditch almost six months after she was abducted. Dru Sjodin has now been dead for seventeen years.

Alphonso Rodriguez Jr. was fifty-three years old when he was convicted of the murder of Dru Sjodin in 2006, three years after her death. He had been released from prison in 2003 after serving twenty-three years for prior crimes, and he was a Level III sex offender. (Level III means that it is likely that he would commit another sex crime.)

Today, Rodriquez is sixty-nine years old and appealing his guilty verdict. His attorneys contend that he is mentally disabled and that he didn't get a fair trial.[52] Of course, there is no recourse for victims, but there are up to five layers of appeal for convicted murderers who are sentenced for federal crimes, and nine layers for those convicted of state crimes.[53]

Dru's mother, Linda Walker, says that she tries to accept the fact that her daughter is dead, and the murderer is still alive, "It was proven in a court of law that he was guilty." It is difficult to be a survivor of a murder victim, whether the perpetrator is apprehended or not.

New Mexico

After I moved to Santa Fe, I got involved in a group called the New Mexico Book Association (NMBA). It's a group of writers, authors, publishers, and others in the book industry. As a result of this affiliation, I was introduced to author Lois Duncan from Albuquerque whose daughter was murdered in 1989. The case was never solved. She wrote a book about her experiences, titled *Who Killed My Daughter?* (1992).

Duncan's daughter, Kaitlyn Arquette, was only eighteen when she was shot in a drive-by shooting on July 16, 1989. The Albuquerque Police hypothesized that it was a random shooting, and that young Kaitlyn was simply in the wrong place at the wrong time.

It's not like the Albuquerque Police Department lacked experience with murder investigations (as the police in Jack's murder). In 2018, there were 12.32/100,000 murders in the city. This compares with 7.97/100,000 in New Mexico and 4.96/100,000 in the US.

Lois always thought the murder was related to Kaitlyn's Vietnamese boyfriend, who was involved with a gang that specialized in drug smuggling and car insurance fraud. The police, however, focused *only* on the possibility of a drive-by, random shooting.

The author blamed inept handling (not due to incompetence, but the myopic idea of what happened, and probably a little "group think"). Law enforcement didn't take the mother's clues and information seriously. Lois Duncan died in 2016, without finding her daughter's murderer.

Kaitlyn's case is still unsolved today. However, in August 2021, Paul Apodaca, now fifty-three, was arrested in Albuquerque on another charge and confessed to killing Kaitlyn Arquette in 1989, along with two other murders. Apodaca was the first person arrested and sentenced in Bernalillio County, New Mexico, under the new sex offender statutes of October 1995. He has been in and out of jail ever since. In an interesting turn of events, Apodaca was on the scene when police investigated the car accident that resulted from shooting Arquette, but the police didn't interview him.

Unresolved

What I share with these unsolved cases is having a family member or friend who is forever gone from this earth, suddenly and without explanation. It is a difficult burden that never really goes away. Another facet of an unsolved murder is the idea that someone killed your loved one, and that person is still living, still free. If the murderer got away with one murder, did they feel emboldened and go on to murder others?

The National Institute of Justice (NIJ) published a paper "Victims of Crime."[54] The NIJ provides funding, events, and training along with data to support local law enforcement. The organization maintains that "The rights of victims are every bit as important as those of alleged criminals."

As a result of the research the NIJ has conducted, the organization knows that victimization may happen to an individual, a family, a group, or a community that has been impacted by a crime. "Victimization also brings significant emotional, psychological, physical, financial, and social consequences." I understand too well!

As I began to put my thoughts on paper (or laptop), I began to think of the reasons why the Wahl murder investigation should be pursued. Simply, I just want the investigation to come to a conclusion, rather than remain an open or unsolved case. Here are some of my reasons:

- Jack's family needs to know whether they knew the murderer or not. What was the murderer's relationship to their son and brother?

- John Nelson's family has remained under a "cloud of doubt" for thirty-five years. John killed himself after being interviewed by law enforcement, yet he didn't claim responsibility in his suicide note. He may have been the last person to have seen Jack alive. Most people would want to confess or clear their conscience prior to shooting themselves. Why didn't he take responsibility?

- The investigators say nothing was missing from Jack's home and that robbery was not the motive. Why would the murderer put him/herself in criminal jeopardy for no reason? Recently, I learned that there *was* something missing: Jack's Concordia class ring has never been found. He always wore it. Was this ring meaningful to the person who killed Jack? Did the murderer take the ring off Jack's hand and keep it as a souvenir?

- It's not fair that the murderer may still be living thirty-five years later, while Jack was taken from his friends and family at age forty-three. Since no one has been held accountable, the murderer could still be alive and enjoying the fact that they got away with it. Did that confidence allow the murderer to go on and murder others?
- The citizens and communities of Cavalier and Pembina County need closure too. After there has been a murder in a small community, where everyone knows each other, it is difficult to go back to feeling safe and secure. Do they still worry when strangers come to town? Do they lock their doors at night? Does the murderer still live among them?
- Jack's friends and family deserve to know whether Jack's social life played a role in his demise. At this point, gossip and innuendo still define what happened that cold February night in 1986, which continues to denigrate Jack's legacy—how he is remembered.

For the past thirty-five years one of the unanswered questions has been, "Was the murder a crime of passion?" Newspaper reports along with the investigators' comments have left that question unanswered. Instead, it leaves intact the implication that Jack had a questionable social life, and that put his life in jeopardy. That kind of thinking puts the blame on Jack himself. That's just not fair.

17. A Different Scenario

IT WASN'T UNTIL I MOVED from Cavalier to Fargo in 1990 that I started to think of a possible suspect in Jack's unsolved murder. One day, after spotting Jim O'Rourke at a Moorhead restaurant, I remembered Jim Salaba saying that he thought O'Rourke was mean, and I then realized that none of the Pembina County law officers involved in the murder investigation would know about his longtime relationship with Jack like I did.

I began to think the investigators' theory may have been partially relevant—homosexuality may have been the seed of a rage that led to Jack's murder—but I don't think it had anything to do with Jack's lifestyle or his parties.

I believe that Jim O'Rourke was homosexual, but I have no definite proof. I know that he never married. And as part of my research for this book, I did communicate with staff at the Rourke Gallery. I asked if Jim O'Rourke was gay and was told, "It's complicated." I also have the information from Joe Knutson, the retired president of Concordia College, who shared that Jim O'Rourke unsuccessfully sought a homosexual relationship with Jack. Obviously, it's unlikely that Jim would murder Jack over a decades-long rejection. But there was another, more recent, possible falling out between the two friends that could lead to a motive.

A Competing Art Gallery

The North Dakota Museum of Art, the state's first art museum, was established by the North Dakota Legislature in 1981. It is located on the UND campus in Grand Forks, in a building where I took physical education classes as a student.

Jack was named to its first board of directors in 1985, a few months before his death, but the grand opening wasn't held until 1989, due to delays with the building renovation. Laurel Reuter, a longtime art instructor at UND, championed this project, and still serves as the executive director, although she plans to retire in December 2021. Jim O'Rourke most likely saw this announcement in 1985 as a threat to his professional and personal relationship with Jack, since Jack was a founding board member of the Rourke Art Gallery; he served in that position until 1981.

After his death, Jack's family left 182 paintings in the care of the North Dakota Museum of Art, according to the *Grand Forks Herald*.[55] I worked with Jack's mother on a guest list for this first showing, which was held in June 1988, at the UND Memorial Union art gallery, since the museum building was still being renovated.

I contacted Reuter as part of the research for this book, but she reported to me that there were no bequests to the museum from either Jack Wahl or his family. I sent her a copy of the *Grand Forks Herald* describing the gift from Jack's estate, but she said that she didn't remember any details. Later, Matt Wallace and Greg Vettel, who currently both work at the ND-MOA, clarified that of the 182 original paintings, thirty-one were exhibited in 1988 and six were donated to the museum's permanent collection. Vettel later added that the family donated ten additional artworks in 2011.

Jack's alliance with the North Dakota Museum of Art at UND may have provided the motivation. I believe that Jim O'Rourke thought Jack would remain loyal to the Rourke Art Gallery by leaving his collection to the Moorhead gallery to control. In Jim O'Rourke's thinking, Jack had developed his interest in art and started collecting art as a result of their relationship, and Jack owed him.

In a full-page story entitled, "James O'Rourke Blends His Art with His Life," a *Grand Forks Herald* writer described the artist as, "soft-spoken, quiet, but he can talk all day about artists and their work." The story centered on O'Rourke's woodcuts and how he surrounded himself with art, at the gallery and at his home, built in 1882 and lovingly restored over several years.[56]

According to the article, O'Rourke was designing a woodcut of his grandparents' farm. He liked to focus on rural landscapes and buildings. The artist originally wanted to be an architect, so his topics combined his love of woodcutting as an art method with buildings and landscapes. O'Rourke's collection of woodcuts at the time of the article was traveling to art galleries and shows throughout the state of North Dakota.

The 1987 *Grand Forks Herald* article also highlighted O'Rourke's accomplishments as a soldier in Europe, his experience as a teacher at three area colleges, and his role as a founding member of the Plains Art Museum in 1975. O'Rourke was fifty-four years old at the time the news story was published.

Art was very important to both Jim O'Rourke and my friend Jack, and art collecting was a bond they shared. That part of Jack's art collection appears to be unaccounted for has always troubled me. I felt suspicious about the fact that Jim controlled the appraisal and inventory of Jack's collection at the time of his death. In 2020, I contacted two of the Wahl siblings and asked one simple question, "What happened to the art collection?" The family was not interested in sharing that information.

*

Everything I've written to this point has been based on fact. My story has relied on my memories, some artifacts, the research I gathered through regional newspaper reports from 1986, and an open-records request filed with the Pembina County Sheriff's Department in October 2020.

The next section of this story is speculation. It is based on what I've seen and heard since the murder. It summarizes what I think *could* have happened at my friend Jack's house after midnight on February 12, 1986, if the investigators had not been so fixated on their initial theory, which appeared to be: (1) Jack Wahl was a homosexual; and (2) the murder was related to his parties and lifestyle, which led to a "gay rage" incident.

A Summary of the Details of the Night of February 12, 1986

Jack lived alone but enjoyed people, so he was sometimes lonely, especially in the evenings. He told me that he had had trouble sleeping lately, although I also knew that he didn't require much sleep. I remember that Jack talked to me about his health, so perhaps that was keeping him awake?

After taking Jean Speckman to her home, Jack stopped at Stu's Pub for a nightcap. It was late—almost midnight when he arrived. John Nelson, a twenty-three-year-old local man, was at Stu's Pub, along with some other bar regulars, primarily young, single men. There were a lot of twenty- to thirty-year-old single males in Cavalier. Most of them liked the small-town lifestyle and worked in a family business or on a family farm somewhere in Pembina County.

Earlier that evening, John Nelson had walked to Stu's Pub from his parents' home, where he lived in the basement. He didn't need a car, since his home was less than a block away. It isn't clear from either the investigation notes or the newspaper reports how long John Nelson had been at Stu's that night, nor how much he had been drinking.

John Nelson was shooting pool with friends when Jack entered the bar, just after midnight. Most of the customers were familiar to Jack, including Bruce, Ken,

Jamie, Bob, Dick, and Roy, all of whom had been bowling next door at Sammy's earlier in the evening. Each of these bar patrons would be interviewed by Pembina County Deputy Alan Latozke as part of a murder investigation the next day.

Two of the other individuals in Stu's Pub were older than the group shooting pool. One was Art Snell, a local citizen and native of Cavalier who was recently divorced. He was well-known for wearing a cowboy hat with a feather. The other was John Bergman from nearby Hoople, North Dakota. He owned a flower shop in Cavalier and was a well-known china painter, a skill that he had learned from his mother. He was very effeminate and probably gay.

Jack sat up at the bar by himself and visited with the bartender, Julie Young, and Art Snell, who sat at the other end of the bar. According to Julie, John Nelson and Jack didn't interact while they were both in the bar, although she added that John, just before he left, had purchased two beers "for the road"—Miller Lite in cans. It was February, and John was wearing a winter coat, so he simply put the unopened beers in his coat pocket.

Jack left just before closing time at 1:00 a.m., and he was alone when he got into his car. He always drove flashy, "one-of-a-kind" cars that were very recognizable. A local policeman, Johnnie Reynolds, noticed him driving around at 1:00 a.m. that night, but he didn't think much of it. The doctor could have been coming from the hospital or clinic, or maybe he was just taking a trip through town to decompress before he went home, as he often did.

Late Night Visitors

Earlier that day, Jack had received a phone call from his old friend Jim O'Rourke, who lived in Moorhead, Minnesota. Jim often stopped in Cavalier on his way to Langdon, North Dakota, to see his parents who still lived there. Jim told Jack that he planned to arrive in Cavalier later that night.

The trip from Moorhead was approximately three hours, and Jim would often make the trip after his art gallery closed for the day. It wasn't unusual that O'Rourke would arrive late in the night. In fact, it was the norm. Perhaps Jim's impending arrival was the reason Jack avoided going home that fateful night and also wanted someone with him?

Sometimes Jim stayed overnight at Jack's house, especially if they had consumed a couple of drinks or the weather was bad. There were two guest rooms in Jack's house, so there was plenty of room for overnight guests. On these occasions, Jim would usually go on to Langdon in the morning when Jack left for work. (Langdon is thirty-five miles due west of Cavalier on State Highway 5.) Jack always let him park in the double garage, especially during the winter, so he wouldn't have to clean the snow off his car in the morning.

Another reason Jim O'Rourke would often stop at Jack's house on his way to Langdon was to return art or pick up art for an upcoming exhibit. Jim didn't drive when he was in Moorhead, but the Rourke Gallery had an old station wagon that he would use for transporting art. He had no personal car, since both his home and the gallery in downtown Moorhead were within walking distance of everything he needed in his daily life, including bars and restaurants. He could even walk to nearby Concordia College for events.

When Jim visited Cavalier, the two old friends would enjoy swapping stories and gossip about the artists they shared as mutual friends. Jack often called me to join them. Sometimes, Jack would pick me up in his car, even though there was only one block between our houses. It was usually late at night—often after 10:00 p.m., so I think he worried about me walking in the dark.

Jack Arrives at Home

When Jack left Stu's Pub, it was almost 1:00 a.m. He drove back toward the Cedar Inn Steakhouse and Lounge to see if anyone he knew was still in the bar. Seeing no one, he drove by the hospital and then found himself on Main Street, or State Highway 18. He saw John Nelson walking home from Stu's Pub and stopped briefly to invite him to his house for a nightcap.

Jack may have wanted someone to come home with him, because he knew Jim O'Rourke would be at his house. Looking back now, I don't think Jack wanted to be alone with Jim. Perhaps John Nelson served the same purpose that I had during previous visits.

John Nelson would have no idea that Jim O'Rourke would be at Jack's house, so perhaps he thought of it as an opportunity to talk to Jack about a loan to buy the bar in Edinburg. John went home and warmed up his car. It was cold that night.

Meanwhile, Jack took another trip down Division Street, or State Highway 5, to see if there was anything going on at Sammy's Bar or The Office, another local bar, but it was a quiet night, and there was no one around. Jack made a U-turn in the Warehouse Grocery parking lot and headed home. John Nelson arrived just as Jack pulled into his garage. Jim O'Rourke's vehicle was already parked inside.

When they entered the house, John Nelson and Jack went directly downstairs, hearing loud voices coming from the television in the family room. Jim O'Rourke was relaxing on the couch, and he had *Deep Throat*, the X-rated movie, running on Jack's television system. Jack introduced the two men and asked John to get a couple of beers from the nearby basement bar. Jim declined to have a drink, saying he was too tired. The three men sat on the U-shaped sectional. The movie continued.

John Nelson didn't know Jim O'Rourke and was surprised when the conversation began with Jim saying, "You're a sneaky son-of-a-bitch. After everything I've done for you, you agree to serve on the fucking board of that new art museum at UND."

O'Rourke was obviously angry with Jack, and John Nelson didn't know quite what to do. Meanwhile, Jack was dozing off on the couch, as he often did after a night of eating, drinking, and socializing. Jack was hardly awake, but Jim continued yelling at him. When Jack didn't respond, Jim fondled the knife in his pocket. He had carried this knife since the day he purchased it while he was stationed in Europe in the '60s.

John was anxious to leave and got up from the couch. O'Rourke ignored him. By now, Jim was pacing

CONNIE L. NELSON   205

behind the sectional near Jack, who was slouched on the couch, either falling asleep or passed out from a night of drinking.

Jim's barrage continued, "You asshole! All the art that you've accumulated as the result of my connections will end up in Grand Forks, at UND? I won't stand for it. You're a traitor." Jack didn't react, which made Jim angrier.

John Nelson was already outside, hoping his car would start. Meanwhile, Jim, who was by now enraged, grabbed the knife in his pocket and began to stab Jack from behind, until Jack finally fell to the floor between the coffee table and the couch. Jim pulled up the light winter jacket that Jack still wore and stabbed him again.

Furious and covered with blood, Jim realized that he had to leave immediately. He hadn't planned to kill Jack, but his temper got the best of him. Shaken by the sight of what he had just done, he threw Jack's winter coat over him like a blanket. Briefly, he thought about all the years he'd known Jack, since meeting at Concordia in the 1960s. As a final act, Jim pulled the Concordia College ring off Jack's hand and put it in his coat pocket.

Jim left the lights on and went up the stairs to the garage entrance off the kitchen. He opened the garage door and started his car. After backing out onto the driveway, he went to the side door and closed the overhead garage door. There would have been footprints in the snow and tire tracks when Jim left the garage. John Nelson would have also left footprints in the same area if he left the house through the garage, but he must have left via the front door, since it was open when the housekeeper arrived the next morning.

Jim was shaking both from the cold and from what had just happened. He knew that his temper had gotten out of control, but this was the worst thing he had ever done. As he drove west down Main Street toward Langdon, he realized that he still had the bloody knife in the pocket of his jacket. He opened the window as he passed the Renwick Dam Recreation Area and threw the knife out the passenger window.

O'Rourke drove toward Langdon, arriving at his parents' home between 2:00 and 3:00 a.m. Using the key he still carried on his key chain, he entered his parents' house without turning on the lights and went to bed.

A Surprise Guest

Most of the people in Cavalier who knew Jack would not have known Jim O'Rourke or anything about their connections over the previous twenty-five years. Even people from the Langdon area might not recognize that James O'Rourke was formerly Jim Rourke of Langdon.

I doubt that any of the law enforcement officers or any member of the legal team involved in the murder investigation would have ever considered Jim O'Rourke as a suspect. They simply wouldn't have known anything about him or his relationship with Jack.

The local investigators fixated on the idea that Jack was homosexual, and since the murder was so violent, it must have been a classic example of "gay rage." I think that whoever killed Jack was angry and had a relationship with him. I also doubt that it was a stranger or a casual acquaintance.

If John Nelson told the investigators that there was a stranger at Jack's house that night, it would have been hard to believe, since most Cavalier residents knew each other. I'm sure John Nelson felt powerless when questioned by Sonny Dump, the BCI investigator, Pembina County Sheriff Wells, and his deputy, Joe Martindale. His inability to shed any light on his brief encounter with O'Rourke, and his awareness that the police saw him as a prime suspect, could certainly have contributed to his suicidal thoughts.

I was not able to review the investigation notes from John Nelson's interview. According to the documentation that I did see, the local people who were interviewed said that I would know some answers. However, I was never questioned. (I have always wished that the original investigators had talked to me.) Yet, when I approached law enforcement members two weeks after the murder to try to talk to them, they basically blew me off. I got the feeling that, just like Lois Duncan in Albuquerque, the cops felt a woman just wouldn't understand.

The local investigators established a scenario regarding what happened that night and were content to build a case based on those initial ideas. (They weren't open-minded.) When John Nelson committed suicide after his lie detector test, it reinforced their theory of what happened, and they never investigated any other leads.

This case has remained "open and inactive" for over thirty-five years. It is not included on the attorney general's list of North Dakota cold cases.

18. Living with Reality

Dead and Gone

THE REALITY OF A STORY like this is that the murderer gets to live another day, while the victim is gone forever. The murderer, even if they are caught, will have more rights than the victim who no longer has a voice or any recourse. The US legal system will exhaust every angle to ensure that the suspect's rights aren't infringed.

Meanwhile, the murderer gets to live, decades longer, while the process runs its course, all on the taxpayer's dime. That isn't fair, is it? That's how it feels: it just isn't fair!

It's a familiar story. After someone dies, you always wish that you had one more opportunity to talk to them, to ask questions and find answers. One of my regrets is that I was so flippant in my conversations with Jack. I didn't know how much he confided in me until he was gone. When he'd worry about his health and tell me he couldn't sleep, I should have asked probing questions. He obviously wanted to talk about it.

Today

How I would love to talk to my friend Jack! Of course, I would want to know what really happened that night, but I would also want to update him on what I've been doing the last thirty-five years. I'm sure he'd like to hear about my kids. I'd love to tell him that I'm a grandma now. He'd get a kick out of my name, "Glamma Connie."

I think my friend Jack would be pleased that as a result of his influence, I am now an art enthusiast and a docent (tour guide) at the Georgia O'Keeffe Museum in Santa Fe, New Mexico.

Since I'm sixty-nine years old this year, it means Jack would be seventy-nine. It's hard to imagine him that age! He's missed so much. Just to put it in perspective and demonstrate how much time has passed since Jack's been gone: I know that he has a niece who is my daughter Sarah's age. They were both born the year Jack died, so he never knew anything about them, and they're already the age I was in 1986 when he was murdered, thirty-four.

I'd like to tell my friend Jack how hard it was to say my son's name after he died. I guess that's why you honor someone by naming a child after them, but I certainly second-guessed that decision for a long time. My daughter loves her brother's name so much that she has always said that if she has a son, she will name him Jack. The name lives on, as do the fond memories.

I would love to talk to Jack's parents, Russell and Dorothy, and find out how they coped with never knowing who killed their first-born son. I can't imagine what that felt like. And I'd like to talk to Jack's sisters and his brother. Did they always wonder if someone they knew murdered their brother? The last time I saw any of them was at the UND Art Show in 1988. I hope there were no arguments over Jack's art collection, and that when they get together, this tragedy doesn't hover like a shadow.

North Dakota is so small that everybody knows each other, especially someone like me, who has lived in five different North Dakota communities. I was told by a Fargo store owner after Jack's death, that his brother returned some Christmas china that had my name on it. There would be no reason that I should have gotten it after Jack died, but it certainly demonstrates my point that virtually everyone knows each other in a small, rural, sparsely populated state like North Dakota. It's difficult to believe with a small population like North Dakota's that someone doesn't know something about Jack's murder. It's even possible the murderer will confess on their deathbed someday.

I'd like to understand why I was meant to cross paths with Joe Knutson, the retired Concordia College president, and Roger Olgard, principal at Lewis & Clark Elementary. Both men reacted when I mentioned that I had lived in Cavalier, North Dakota. They both asked me if I knew Jack. In a way, it was a nice connection, but at the time it made me sad. Both individuals died before I could follow-up with them and ask questions.

After many interactions with Jim O'Rourke when I lived in Fargo, I am convinced that he had the incentive to kill Jack. He wanted Jack's art collection for the Rourke Gallery in Moorhead, Minnesota. He was always very nervous when I'd remind him that I knew him through Jack and that I had met him in Cavalier. Jim O'Rourke would be one person who could have appreciated Jack's Concordia ring too. (They were both Concordia grads.)

I would like to ask Jim O'Rourke about the art that disappeared from my house after the murder, and I'd like to know where Jack's collection of art went after he died. Since Jim O'Rourke died in 2011, I'll never have a chance to talk to him, but I do intend to find the answer about where Jack's art collection ended up.

Jim Salaba had told me one time that Jim O'Rourke was "mean." It was interesting to see the comments about Jim O'Rourke from his colleagues following his death. "Mean" was a theme that jumped out at me and brought back Jim Salaba's comment again.

John Nelson is someone I never met during my residence in Cavalier. His suicide note intrigues me. I wonder if he told the investigators that someone else was at Jack's house that fateful night. Since he was young, and in the company of people with more power than he possessed, I believe he felt that no one would believe him.

If my theory about the murderer is correct, I don't believe that law enforcement officers in Pembina County would have known anything about Jim O'Rourke. In addition, I don't think that they knew how much time I spent with Jack. They should have asked me. I wish that the investigators would have been more open-minded, dug deeper, and asked more questions.

Closure

Today I am retired and a grandmother, with two healthy children who are both happily married and have children of their own. I am finally putting my feelings down on paper. Maybe thirty-five years after my friend Jack was murdered, I can put away the anger and denial and finally *accept* that I lived through a traumatic experience, and that I am a survivor.

Appendix I: Postscript

Oliver Gregory, my father-in-law, divorced Marge and moved back to Cavalier, but he was having health problems by then and didn't live at home long. Oliver eventually moved to a nursing home, where he died in 2018. His home was sold to a young, local couple.

Jack's home has had a couple of different owners, and the Tareen family has moved to Minneapolis. Now retired, Dr. Jamil Tareen, age eighty-two, and his family are involved in medical work in Pakistan as volunteers.

Glenn Wells died at age eighty-seven in the local nursing home. He was the Pembina County sheriff from 1959-1986. Tributes in his obituary described him as honest and friendly. My father-in-law, Oliver Gregory, and my ex-husband and his brother were all listed as pallbearers for his funeral, held at one of the local Lutheran churches, on May 25, 2009.

James J. "Joe" Martindale became a deputy under Sheriff Wells in 1969 and succeeded Glenn Wells as Pembina County sheriff in 1987. Joe retired in 2003 and moved to Fargo. He died in 2013.

My ex-husband lives in Grand Forks, North Dakota, where my son Jack helps him to live independently with Parkinson's disease.

Appendix II: Apology

I want to apologize in advance to each of the people who are mentioned in this book who are no longer living. They can't defend themselves. I felt that it was important to tell my story anyway.

- John Nelson, suspect—died by suicide in March 1986.
- Joe Knutson, retired president, Concordia College—died 1992.
- Jean Speckman, friend of Jack's who had dinner with him the night before he died; a widow—died 1993.
- Arvid Benson and his twin sister Dorothy Wahl—both died in 2001. Arvid was Jack's uncle who lived in Moorhead; Dorothy was Jack's mother.
- Roger Olgard, originally from Hannaford, North Dakota, Jack's hometown, the principal at Lewis & Clark, where my kids attended elementary school—died 2003.
- Johnnie Reynolds, the local cop in Cavalier (1970-1995)—died in 2008.
- Glenn Wells, the Pembina County sheriff (1959-1986)—died in 2009.
- E.F. "Sonny" Dump, North Dakota BCI investigator (1947-2009)—died in 2009.
- Russell Wahl, Jack's father—died in 2010.

- Patty Benson, Jack's aunt in Moorhead (married to Arvid)—died in 2010.
- Jim O'Rourke, executive director of the Rourke Museum, Moorhead—died after a fall in 2011.
- Joe Martindale, deputy sheriff of Pembina County and later sheriff (1987-2002)—died in 2013.
- Neil Fleming, local attorney and president of the Pembina County Hospital Board—died in 2017.
- Annette Hughes, nanny for Jack and Sarah Gregory—died in California in March 2017.
- Oliver Gregory, local car dealer and my father-in-law (1979-1990)—died in 2018.
- Dean Becker, an influential source in the investigation—died in an ATV accident on Friday, April 13, 2018.
- Dr. E. J. Larson, local physician—died 8/26/2021.

Appendix III: Five Unsolved North Dakota Murders

The Wahl murder is not the only unsolved case in North Dakota. I've selected the following five cases as a sample, simply because I remembered the news stories about them:[57]

Kenneth Engy (a.k.a. Kenneth Nygaard) was found dead in his garage in Edmore, North Dakota, in October 1988. At first the investigators thought he died from carbon monoxide poisoning, but the authorities also learned that he'd had a fight in a bar with a coworker the night he died. The family believes that Curtis Heck is responsible.

Nineteen-year-old **Russell Turcotte** from Wolf Point, Montana, never made it home after calling his mother from Grand Forks, North Dakota, in July 2002. He was missing for four months when a farmer found his naked body in a tree stand near Devils Lake, one hundred miles to the west of Grand Forks. All that is known is that he died from blunt force trauma to the back of his head.

This case remains under the jurisdiction of North Dakota's Ramsey County, with assistance from the Bureau of Criminal Investigations. At one time, the FBI considered Joseph Edward Duncan III, a convicted murderer and sex offender, but he was never declared a suspect. Turcotte's mother, Linda Hansen, still contends that law enforcement was too slow to react. The family was told to file a missing-person's report in Montana.

Hansen wishes that the Grand Forks Police had taken her call for help more seriously. She worries that whoever killed her son has hurt others too. She also worries that the murderer is still looking for other victims.[58]

In 1987, **Kathy Bonderson** left her home in New Rockford, North Dakota, to look for her teenage son, and she never returned home. The next morning, her car was found totally burned, with her inside. At first, it appeared that she had simply crashed her car. Then in 2005, a new autopsy was performed, and evidence of murder was discovered.

Norman Limesand was killed over a water dispute near Bismarck, North Dakota, in 1999. He had confronted someone named Steven Thomas, who pleaded guilty to the murder three years later, and he served ten years in prison. However, Limesand's body is still missing.

Anita Knutson was found stabbed to death in her apartment in Minot on June 4, 2007. A blood-covered knife was found in the sink. There was no sign of a break-in. The case is still unsolved.

Each of these unsolved murders took place in a different part of the state, so it is difficult to blame law enforcement for ineptitude, unless of course you blame the state of North Dakota's law enforcement system in total. Instead, I believe that murder is so rare in this sparsely populated state that law enforcement simply has little experience.

These five unsolved murders took place over a twenty-year period, 1987-2007. North Dakota didn't have a cold case program until November 2005. Attorney General Wayne Stenehjem launched the cold case project when new technology made reopening unsolved murders and solving them a possibility.

The Bonderson case was one of the first cold cases reopened. A new autopsy was ordered, and as a result, the investigators discovered that Kathy Bonderson was murdered, and her car was set on fire afterward.

Thankfully, Kathy Bonderson's unsolved death was pursued. New evidence proved that she was murdered. Investigators named her husband as the most likely suspect. Her husband vanished after the case was reopened and later committed suicide. When the primary suspect has died there is no one to charge. It's the end of the line, except for the questions: If Kathy's husband did plan and execute Kathy's murder, how was he able to keep his secret from 1987 until 2005 when the case was reopened? How did he live with himself?

Family and friends always hope for a final resolution, whether the case goes to trial or not. They want to know what happened, even if there isn't a happy ending. For example:

- I'm sure Kenneth Engy's family has a difficult time whenever Curtis Heck is nearby. What does Curtis Heck think took place in Kenneth's garage? Or does he know what happened?
- Russell Turcotte was just a kid. Did he decide to hitchhike home to Wolf Point,

Montana, when his mother failed to send money for his travel? Did he get picked up by someone with ulterior motives? His body was simply discarded. He lay there in that cold tree stand for four months until a farmer found the naked body. What a way to end a life! Who could do this to another human being?

- Steven Thomas admitted to killing Norman Limesand but can't remember where he put the body. Limesand's family must wonder if his body will ever be found. It's been over twenty years since his murder. Steven Thomas has served jail time for this crime, but he has been released, and Norman is still dead and missing. Is that fair?

- Who wanted to kill Anita Knutson in her Minot apartment? Whoever the killer was, they got in and out of the apartment without being seen. By 2007, there was DNA testing. The murderer left the murder weapon behind in the kitchen sink. Did the murderer leave no DNA evidence behind? Is the murderer still living in Minot?

Appendix IV: Letters to the Editor

A series of letters to the editor were published in the *Grand Forks Herald* following the Wahl murder.

Article didn't do justice to Dr. Wahl of Cavalier

CAVALIER, N.D. — This letter is a response to the Feb. 15 Herald article by Ann Bailey on Dr. Jack Wahl's death.

In my opinion, the article is a piece of trash fit for publications that are sold at grocery store checkouts. Once the Herald went beyond the known facts of the case, it became pornography, an exploitation of rumors and gossip. It is simply irresponsible journalism.

The Herald should be ashamed. Your quotes from "five individuals, including one who talked to Wahl the night before he died" were largely exaggerations on the part of these unnamed sources. This is evidenced by the fact that none had their names printed, nor was it stated where the bartender worked.

The reporter twice tried to contact my bartender, Julie Young. Julie called me after the initial contact for advice. I advised her not to say anything. Later the reporter entered my establishment and again asked Julie for information; she declined, at which point the reporter left and presumably went to another bar and interviewed the bartender there.

The Herald should stick to its job and report the facts that satisfy the people's right to know. It should not print small-town gossip, which seldom contains a grain of truth and which appeals strictly to people's base interests, nothing more. Small-town gossip is 99 percent exaggeration and 1 percent truth. That is a fact the Herald can depend on. Small-town gossip printed comes very close to being slander.

Jack Wahl should be remembered for the good things he accomplished.

mail bag

He was an asset to our community and loved by all. He was a sensitive, caring individual, evidenced by his thriving medical practice. His death affects all of us and he will be deeply missed by this community.

I am not sure what intent the Herald had when it printed this article, and I feel it should explain its motives. I also think the Herald owes Julie Young an apology, since it appears that she was the bartender quoted.

Finally, the name of my establishment is Stu's Pub, not Stu's Bar, as has been printed in three articles.

In the future, I suggest you get the facts straight, and stick to the facts.

Stuart Askew

Askew is the owner of Stu's Pub. The Herald writer visited a different bar before stopping at Stu's. The Herald article did not quote Julie Young. — The editor.

□ □ □

CRYSTAL, N.D. — I read with disgust and great concern one of the lead stories in the Saturday edition of the Herald pertaining to the death of Dr. John D. Wahl of Cavalier.

The questions that were asked and the answers given had nothing to do with this death. We had a terrible tragedy happen and all who knew him loved him and were crushed by this bizarre murder.

My big question — why was this information obtained from a bar? Why didn't the reporter go to some of his co-workers, friends or even patients? He was thought of highly by all the elderly, and made his weekly visits to an area home, where these elderly folks could hardly wait for him to come. He catered to the elderly and was so kind and thoughtful to this age group.

I speak as a patient and feel that the Herald has done a terrible injustice to a person who did so much for everybody. We have lost a man in his prime of life and one who had so many years left to continue his good-doing. What Wahl did at his home or on his days or hours off was nobody's business. To have this junk printed after he is gone is a great injustice.

I can only say that in the future, please contact the people who can give information that will be more complimentary and not with the idea of dragging down someone who was charitable and did so much for his community and the outlying area.

We have lost a dedicated physician and a compassionate friend. Our sincere sympathy to the family of Dr. John D. Wahl.

Anna Marie Strand

Won't you write?

Letters are welcome. Signature, address and phone number where the writer can be reached during the day are required. Letters are subject to editing.

Address: Mail Bag, Grand Forks Herald, P.O. Box 998, Grand Forks, N.D. 58206-0998.

A small town hurts after doctor's death

Lynn Schroeder, editor of the Cavalier, N.D., Chronicle, said in his column, "Just Wanted To Say," on Tuesday:

Have you noticed how much different Cavalier feels lately? Tough to describe it . . . just different. Everything's just a little out of place. Everyone's just a little on edge. I guess tragedies, nearly back-to-back, have that effect on a small town.

The big city people don't notice it much. They live with it every day. Cities like New York, Chicago, Los Angeles, treat fires and murder as daily occurances, just another annoyance. But here, in Cavalier, these incidents are not simply glanced over. Oh, we're not completely shaken or torn apart, as some of the media would want to believe, but we're not nonchalant about it either.

A fire a couple of week ago was big excitement in this area. It gave us a front page story and gave everyone something to gossip about for awhile. Now we realize that a part of Cavalier's history is no longer with us and can never return to us again.

Last Thursday brought an even greater tragedy to our town. A human life was taken. Dr. John (Jack) Wahl, friend, doctor and colleague of many, was found stabbed to death in his own home.

In the newspaper business, a murder is, like it or not, front page news.

I hope none of you were planning on reading a lot of dirt about Doc Wahl's life. I had read and heard these types of reports, about the doctor's social life in this area's daily paper (the Grand Forks Herald) and on the TV newscasts, and quite frankly, I found it very distasteful. The only good the information did was to stretch the story to the limit. To me, that info is too personal and should remain in the memories of his friends, not splattered on Page One or a TV screen by reporters who didn't even know what he looked like until they borrowed a picture from our files.

I'm afraid all you're going to get from the Chronicle is the facts. As boring as that may be, that's all. I realize this is unheard of in this day and age of news-reporting values, but the longer I work here the more I realize that some of the old values are still some of the best.

Cavalier, N.D., my hometown. Oh, I'm still proud of it and I'll always think it's a great place to live and work, but now, it's different. Not bad or anything. Just different.

their opinion

Aquino profoundly short of experience

The Daily Telegraph of London said in an editorial last week:

Mr. Reagan wants to prevent the communists coming out of the jungle and into power. So do most people, including a great majority of the Philippine people. He must understand that the mechanism for keeping them out is not Ferdinand Marcos. No one is being naive about an Aquino government. Corazon Aquino is profoundly short of experience. She will no doubt fulfill her quota of silly decisions. But she was elected; the people chose her. Only eight days of rigging and stealing so gross as to make government-appointed tellers walk out of the count now obstruct her. New elections are required.

The ultimate boat person

The Bismarck Tribune said in an editorial Wednesday:

France and the United States have administered the right prescription for "Baby Doc" Duvalier — quarantine. Isolating vicious despots who plague this world is no sure cure for dictatorship, but at least it makes the politics of democracy look healthier . . . Besides, there's something appealing about the idea of a penniless Duvalier spending the rest of his days in a boat, going from nation to nation in search of refuge.

Winter in Hawaii

Ken Rogers, editor of the Mandan, N.D., News, said in his opinion column Sunday:

The Blue Cross, Blue Shield Board of directors had their monthly meeting in Maui. (That is Hawaii for those of you with little money to burn after paying for your health insurance.) Do you think "insensitive" is too strong? How about "arrogant" or "incredibly bad taste." Somehow, and I really don't understand why, the Blue Cross, Blue Shield board has not gotten the message about keeping medical costs under control. It is not so much the $50,000 they spent having the meeting (small change for the health insurance people), but the gall. Hell, what's power for if you never get to abuse it!

Editorials from other newspapers appear Fridays on the Herald's editorial page.

Mail bag

Wahl story offended community

HAMILTON, N.D. — The Herald has managed to anger an entire community, upset an already bereaved family and upset me enough to write this.

Your story about Dr. John D. Wahl's murder published last Saturday contained accounts of his personal life that were totally uncalled for. You had a top-notch news story, but managed to make it a fourth-rate account by adding gossip that had no bearing on the news story. Facts, if indeed they were facts, about Dr. Wahl's personal life were totally irrelevant.

Never in my life have I heard a newspaper article referred to in a funeral sermon. Your story was — by the minister who gave Dr. Wahl's funeral service. The minister very eloquently reminded those present of the Herald's total insensitivity. Had it not been a funeral service, his words would have prompted a standing ovation.

I realize that you are obligated to report the relevant facts. Why did you have to dredge out the irrelevant gossip?

Dr. Wahl had many friends in the Cavalier community. You have many subscribers there. You have angered them and dismayed them by your lack of tact. I assure you that your reporters' questions in the future will

be met with a lot more "no comment," or perhaps something much more descriptive.

Wes Argue

□□□

WALHALLA, N.D. — You offended a countless number of people with your front-page publication regarding Dr. Wahl at the time of his cruel death.

His marital status and the unbelievably distorted portrayal of his personal and social life were irrelevant to his competence as a physician.

I, too, would fall asleep had I been up all night because of an emergency or OB case, was on call or had a strenuous day at the clinic and hospital.

Dr. Wahl is remembered with high esteem in this corner of the state. He was a very capable, compassionate, generous and friendly man. He did not deserve, nor did his family, some of the coverage given by the news media.

Molly Nelson

Good farm editorial

GRAFTON, N.D. — The Herald was absolutely correct in its assessment of the 50 percent-92 percent provision of the new farm bill ("Congress monkeys with too many crops," Herald opinion, Feb. 17). If enacted, such a provision will destroy the markets for most of the free market crops in this country. The end result will simply force more farmers in financial difficulties as their markets are destroyed through oversupply.

As Jim Durkin noted in the editorial, the provision will be particularly devastating for potato and bean farmers in the valley. If sunflower

producers need more production, they either should bid up the market price or get a direct subsidy, if they can justify it. They certainly should not do it through the back door with a program that will destroy other markets.

I hope the editorial is read by our congressional delegation, and that they do everything they can to remove this provision from the farm bill.

Ralph Kingsbury

Kingsbury is president of the Walsh County Farm Bureau.

Enough!

PARK RIVER, N.D. — Our president is more concerned about his latest stage production in Grenada and our senators are more concerned about re-election than the survival of our farmers. The farmers' problems are the result of listening to Washington instead of relying on their own intuition. If they could set prices like the Big Three defense contactors, they would all be rich today.

We have poured $74 million into Grenada (population 100,000), millions into the Philippines and millions to every tin dictator around the world who professes to be fighting communism. Enough is enough!

The farmers of this country are about the only thing that has worked well for the United States. It's time our deadwood senators got off the pot and put a five-year moratorium on farm foreclosures, and you can pull the bucks out of the foolish defense program to do it.

George W. Cook

2-23-86

Stealing a town's grief

By Mike Jacobs

Our coverage of the death of John Wahl, the Cavalier physician found dead in his home on Feb. 13, has drawn the harshest criticism I've had to deal with as editor of the Herald. We printed letters Friday and Saturday, some of them bitterly critical of the Herald and its reporter.

matters at hand

Ann Bailey, whose name appeared on the story published Feb. 15, did what she was trained to do, what we told her to do, what we expect her to do and what we pay her to do. She went to Cavalier and she gathered the information she could about Dr. Wahl and the circumstances of his death. She came back to Grand Forks with the information and she wrote a story.

I decided what to print. I mean that literally. I came to the Herald after the Sioux hockey game on Feb. 14 and I edited Bailey's story, deleting some material and asking for better documentation of other material. This process is not unusual, although I don't often get directly involved in it.

Readers have said that the decisions I made resulted in coverage that was irrelevant and insensitive. I understand the criticism. I hope readers will understand why these decisions were made.

We had printed a great deal of material indicating that Wahl was popular in Cavalier — especially on Feb. 14, the day after his body was found. Bailey and regional reporter Mike Brue wrote that story. Bailey was in Cavalier and Brue used the telephone to call people who knew Wahl.

Bailey learned about another part of Wahl's life when she returned to Cavalier that day — a part of Wahl's life that suggested why he might have been the victim of a shocking crime. I don't think that information was irrelevant. Investigation of any murder would uncover personal information

about the victim. So far, no one has disputed that what was printed is true. Some said it was exaggerated and represented only a small part of his life. Some read what was printed and imagined a great deal more that was not printed.

Some of the reaction focused on the anonymity of the five people who were sources of the information in the article. I felt that was justified in this case, because it was the only way to present the information. Some reaction was against quoting a bartender who was interviewed in a bar. My own perspective is that bartending is a respectable occupation and that it's as natural to interview a bartender in a bar as it is to interview a newspaper editor in a newspaper office or a farmer on a farm. I thought identifying the person as the report of Wahl's activities. Unfortunately, giving an occupation started speculation about who might have provided the information and in a small town that could lead to identification of the source. To provide real anonymity we should have left out the person's occupation.

Some reaction was against publishing any material at all, no matter how it was gathered. Some people from Cavalier felt that publishing the information was a kind of invasion. Cavalier's privacy was invaded, its peace disturbed and some of its assumptions wrecked. But the newspaper didn't do that; the crime did that.

The publicity did something else. It stole the community's grief. Printing the material on Saturday meant the people of Cavalier didn't have a chance to mourn the loss of their doctor, an important man and a friend, before other parts of his life were analyzed — parts that they didn't know about, or that they knew about and accepted because they valued him so much.

I feel bad about that and I'm sorry we had to print the material when we did. I know it caused pain in Cavalier because I grew up in a town a lot like Cavalier, just a little farther west.

But the people of Cavalier have to understand that even more attention could be paid to their town and to Wahl's life as the investigation goes on. It can't be any other way.

I'm not asking people in Cavalier to agree with me, only to understand why we did what we did, and why I feel the way I do about it.

I'll try to explain this in person in Cavalier. I'll buy coffee for anyone who comes to Thompson's Cafe in Cavalier between 9 a.m. and 11 a.m. on Thursday. I'll listen to comments and answer questions.

□ □ □

Jacobs is editor of the Herald. You can ask questions or make comments about the Herald by calling him at 780-1103 in Grand Forks, 1 (800) 732-4293 in North Dakota or 1 (800) 437-5317 in Minnesota. Or write Jacobs at the Herald, Box 998, Grand Forks, N.D. 58206-0998.

More thoughts about Wahl murder story

EAST GRAND FORKS — Is the Herald insensitive to Cavalier's feelings? Insensitive to Dr. John Wahl's family? Go a little further — were they insensitive to John Rairdon and his family? Are they insensitive to you and me when they print the court proceedings, bankruptcies, divorces and all the other pain that exists? I believe the sensitivity is within us. The pain, the shame and guilt is there, and now it is forced out of the closet.

Small towns, large families and relationships are a lot alike. When part of them is in pain, the whole unit trembles.

My sympathies are to Wahl's family and friends and to all of us who suffer when the Herald prints a story that makes our private lives public. It's important at that time to find a support system and go on with our lives. When the news story hits home, it's time to address the issue; the fact that we are so uncomfortable with the story should tell us something.

Remember, too, that as the story unfolds, other facts will be told and there probably will be more pain.

I wonder, though, if Cavalier is not biased toward the "good folk." If Wahl were poor, transient or young, would it hurt so much?

We feel anger and pain when someone we love is exposed — the bad along with the good. It seems obvious to me that Wahl was loved by many.

The Grand Forks Herald must always remember that it serves a unique population — many small towns, many families and many humans. I believe the Herald trips far more often than we'll ever know.

Bette Driscoll

□□□

ROSEAU, Minn. — I read with great interest the letters of Stewart Askew and Anna Marie Strand in the Friday Herald. Also the excerpt of Lynn Schroeder from the Cavalier Chronicle (Their opinion, Feb. 21). I agree with the gist of these letters and the excerpts. Even the main reporters of ABC

mail bag

(Peter Jennings, etc.) bring their interpretation of the news, and not the news as it really is. I don't like it!

But today I want to contribute something in memory of Dr. Wahl. As was stated in the above-mentioned letters, he was a very considerate person, a very kind person and a great doctor.

I feel Dr. Wahl really saved my life, in helping diagnose my aneurism in time. Had it ruptured, it could have meant instant death. I always will remember him as a very special person.

So again, my hat is off to Stuart, Anna Marie and Lynn. May God bless them and may Dr. Wahl's soul rest in peace. Amen.

Lyell P. Miller

□□□

DRAYTON, N.D. — Perhaps the type of reporting done by the Herald on the Cavalier incident should be a lesson to other communities in the area. A "no comment" answer to any inquiries from the Herald reporters would seem to be the safest reply. Depend on the local paper for local news. The Herald seems to stress the more sordid or sensational side of the news.

To even mention Dr. Wahl's private life is at this time irrelevant. An editor can always say, "We had to print it," but what was really gained? Our area of the state has lost a fine, compassionate doctor — we know from past experience at the Cavalier Clinic and nursing home.

Frances Weinlaeder

Won't you write?

Letters are welcome, preferably of no more than 200 words. Signature, address and phone number where the writer can be reached during the day are required. Letters are subject to editing.

Address: Mail Bag, Grand Forks Herald, P.O. Box 998, Grand Forks, N.D. 58206-0998.

2-26-86

Cavalier meeting went well

By Mike Jacobs

Straight to the questions this week. Number one: How did it go in Cavalier?

matters at hand

This follows last week's column, and it comes from several readers (more than I realized took the time to read what I have to say on Sunday mornings).

It went well in Cavalier.

I went there on Thursday morning to talk with townspeople about the Herald's coverage of the murder of John Wahl, a popular Cavalier doctor. About 45 people showed up, although not all of them stayed the whole two hours.

The discussion was friendly and the questions and comments were thoughtful.

Some people obviously were hurt deeply by what the Herald had said about Wahl and argued that it wasn't true. Some conceded that it might be true but argued that it wasn't relevant. Some said it was true and relevant but wasn't nice and shouldn't have been printed. Some understood why we printed it and one pressed for even more details. Many wanted to know what we'll do next.

I said that we had thought carefully about what we printed and that our decision was not malicious. I said that murder always exposes the victim and the community, and that publicity is part of the tragedy.

I also said that I do not consider the Herald's coverage to be prize-winning journalism but that I'm comfort-

I said that we had thought carefully about what we printed and that our decision was not malicious. I said that murder always exposes the victim and the community, and that publicity is part of the tragedy.

I also said that I do not consider the Herald's coverage to be prize-winning journalism but that I'm comfortable defending our stories. I conceded that there would have been many other ways to approach the story.

It is obvious that there is a great deal of pain in Cavalier and I hope that our meeting helped people deal with their shock and grief and anger. A minister who attended said it probably would. The minister also suggested that people reacted strongly to our stories because anger is part of the grieving process. No one knows who to blame for the murder, the minister said, so anger was directed at the Herald.

□ □ □

Follow-up: What will the Herald do next?

I told people at the meeting that our staff is working on a profile of Dr. Wahl that will give as complete a picture of his life as possible. As part of that article, we hope to report the last hours of his life as well as we can. We also will continue to cover the investigation. I said at the meeting that information about the investigation will help to dispel rumors about what might have happened and I urged law enforcement officials to be more forthcoming with information about their efforts. I put the same argument to them in a letter.

It is not the Herald's role to try to solve this crime; law enforcement can handle that job. Our role is to report what happened as completely as we can. Sharing information is the only way any of us will ever be able to understand this tragedy.

□ □ □

Thursday's session in Cavalier was successful enough that I've decided to wander into another hotbed of criticism of the Herald: the UND campus.

City Editor John Vanvig and I will take a big table in the Varsity Inn in the Memorial Union on Thursday at 1:30 p.m. We'll buy coffee for anyone who wants to talk about the Herald.

□ □ □

In admiration of Dr. Wahl

mail bag

PEMBINA, N.D. — This is another letter in response to the story on Dr. John Wahl and a letter to Ann Landers in the Herald a few days after the murder of Dr. Wahl. Someone complained to Landers about doctors never being available or caring. My letter is in response to both articles.

Dr. Wahl was my family doctor for 16 years. He delivered my five children, two on his day off and only one during office hours. He saw me through 14 years of children with colds, flu, infections, accidents and other child-related illness and hospitalizations.

Our communities are full of people who will truly miss our doctor, who was always there to make each visit so personal. We will not find a family doctor, friend, community servant and counselor to replace Dr. Wahl.

Perhaps we all deserve a slap on the hands for what we do in our off hours, but do we want them slapped in public? Would we care to have our off hours or our business hours and personal accomplishments published if the Herald were writing about us?

We are all humans who God allows to make personal choices, and perhaps we sometimes tend to forget that doctors fall in the human category, also.

On judging others, the Bible tells us in Matthew 7:3,5, "Why look at the speck in your brother's eye when you can't see past the log in your own? You hypocrite! First take the log out of your own eye and then you will be able to see clearly to take the speck out of your brother's eye" ("Good News" version).

Maybe we all need to take a closer look at our own personal lives before we pay so much attention to someone else's!

P.S. Editor! At the top of your page each day, it says, "It will be the people's paper run strictly in their interests." Perhaps pay more attention to "their interests."

Patty Morin

□ □ □

HOOPLE, N.D. — I am writing to extend my sympathy to the family of Dr. John Wahl on behalf of the thousands of people who new and trusted him as their doctor and friend. He was one of the kindest and most trusted of any man I have ever known.

He was the primary doctor to four generations of my family. Not only was he a very competent physician, but had that rare gift of magic in his personality that enabled him to be instantly liked and trusted by people ranging in age from 2 to 92. He genuinely cared about people he came in contact with, regardless of their position or financial status. He had a rare talent for knowing and being concerned with the welfare of people.

He could make anyone laugh with his great sense of humor, especially the elderly, who in many cases didn't have much to laugh about. My grandmother thought the world of him, as he could always make things seem better to her.

The community of Cavalier, as well as a large area around Cavalier, has lost a great deal more than a physician. We have lost a friend, leader and a great personality. This is the personal life that most of us will choose to remember.

Joel Anderson

□ □ □

COOPERSTOWN, N.D. — I've lost a young friend, one I had known since his grade school days in Hannaford. As he attained success in his chosen profession, I saw him less frequently, but the bond of family friendship remained.

I held Doctor John in high esteem (I never called him Jack). I hold him in high esteem still, and deeply regret the tragedy that took his life. To those who point an accusing finger, I say, Look deeply into your hearts and minds and ask yourselves whether every facet of your personal and private life could withstand the searing rays of public scrutiny?

St. Paul said it well, "Whatsoever things are lovely and of good report. If there be any virtue, think on these things." There was much that was virtous about Doctor John. He had time and patience for many who in the biblical sense would be classes as "the least of these." Our creator will weigh each one of us in the balance when our time comes. In the final analysis, his is the only opinion that really matters.

The grieving family deserves our prayerful support and compassion.

Margorie Troseth

Why invite racists?

GRAND FORKS — In response to the Feb. 19 editorial suggesting that UND's symposium on South Africa should have had a representative from the South African government, I would argue that it seems wrong to invite racists from that government to a symposium sponsored in part by the UND Peace Studies Program.

If you are inviting scientists to take part in a discussion on the exact shape of the world, you would most likely invite one who said that the world is round, but it would not make sense to invite a scientist who insists that the world is flat. The reason for this is that the theory that the world is flat is wrong, just as racism in the form of apartheid is wrong.

Why should we pay for racists to come here and make excuses for their actions, when the stories that need to be heard are those of the victims?

Eagle Glassheim

Glassheim is a student at Central High School.

Won't you write?

Letters are welcome, preferably of no more than 200 words. Signature, address and phone number where the writer can be reached during the day are required. Letters are subject to editing.

Address: Mail Bag, Grand Forks Herald, P.O. Box 998, Grand Forks N.D. 58206-0998.

3-3-86

Wahl stories excellent

CRYSTAL, N.D. — I was one of the first to complain about a story appearing in the Herald a couple of weeks ago. Now I want to be one of the first to compliment you on one of the finest stories I have ever read in any paper.

The story about Dr. John Wahl in your edition last Sunday was excellent. You paid a great tribute to a great man. It was so good to hear what his friends and colleagues had to say about him and interesting to read all about his fine art collection.

My thanks on behalf of hundreds of other people on this great reporting.

Anna Marie Strand

3-30-86

The region

Grand Forks Herald

The Helper

Dorothy Abrahamson

A sampler of the year

This sampler of the top local news stories for 1986 was chosen by Herald editors.

Reagan comes to town

Rumors began circulating in early October that the president would pay

three weeks later, Andrews lost the election.

Taylor loses, wins, loses

As 1986 drew to a close, a jury of his peers found Grand Forks County Sheriff Gordon Taylor not guilty of

der.

Battle against nuclea

widespread opposition gr U.S. Energy Department's a ment Jan. 16 that four nort Minnesota areas were und

Wednesday ★

December 31, 1986

top local stories

Cavalier doctor stabbed

Dr. John Wahl, a popular physician in the Cavalier area, was found dead in his basement Feb. 13, and authorities said he died of multiple stab wounds. Investigators were left with few leads, and by the year's end the case remained "open but inactive."

Appendix V: Bibliographyv

Recommended Reading

Duncan, Lois (2012). *Who Killed My Daughter? The Startling True Story of a Mother's Search for Her Daughter's Murderer.* Open Road Integrated Media.

Kuhta, Alvina (2021). *Crime in Rural and Small Towns: True Stories Collection of Unsolved Murders and Other Bad Things: Criminal Case Studies.* Amazon Kindle.

Little, John (2018). *Who Killed Tom Thomson? The Truth about the Murder of One of the Twentieth Century's Most Famous Artists.* Skyhorse Publishing.

Metalious, Grace (1956). *Peyton Place.* Simon & Schuster.

Miller, Chanel (2019). *Know My Name.* Penguin Books.

Moore, Paula (2008). *Cricket in the Web: The 1949 Unsolved Murder that Unraveled Politics in New Mexico.* UNM Press.

Morris, Rebecca (2018). *A Murder in My Hometown.* WildBlue Press.

Schuler, Rita Lt. (2021). *The Low Country Murder of Gwendolyn Elaine Fogel: A Cold Case Solved.* History Press.

Toth, Emily (1981; reprinted 1999). *Inside Peyton Place: The Life of Grace Metalious.* University Press of Mississippi.

Books about Writing and Publishing

King, Stephen (2000). *On Writing: A Memoir of the Craft*. Simon & Schuster.

Neighbour, Mary E. (2020). *Self-Publishing Wizard or Wannabe: How to Hire the Best Editor, Designer, or Book Guide*. Upriver Downriver Books.

Sedwick, Helen (2017). *Self-Publisher's Legal Handbook*, second edition. Ten Gallon Press.

Zinsser, William (2006). *On Writing Well: The Classic Guide to Writing Non-Fiction*. Harper Collins.

Endnotes

1   The National Association of Memoir Writers
newsletter, retrieved May 20, 2021, https://
www.namw.org/.

2   The *Forum*, March 23, 2021, p. B-5.

3   *Grand Forks Herald*, March 23, 1986, p. 9-A.

4   *Fondly We Remember*, published by the
Hamilton Book Committee, Hamilton, North
Dakota (1980), pp. 68-69.

5   "A Timeline of HIV and AIDS," https://
www.hiv.gov/hiv-basics/overview/history/
hiv-and-aids-timeline.

6   She died in California in March 2017, where
she was living with her son, John.

7   The percentages listed here reflect the 994
autopsies performed in North Dakota during
the 2017-2019 Biennium (the most recent
report).

8   Investigation notes, interview with the
Cavalier Clinic physicians, February 16, 1986.
David Lybeck, North Dakota BCI; Homicide
Case #09-86-0004.

9   Investigation notes, interview with the
Cavalier Clinic physicians, February 16, 1986.
David Lybeck, North Dakota BCI; Homicide
Case #09-86-0004.

10   Investigation notes, interview with the

Cavalier Clinic physicians, February 16, 1986. David Lybeck, North Dakota BCI; Homicide Case #09-86-0004.

11 Investigation notes, interview with Ken Askew (undated), by Pembina County Deputy Sheriff Joe Martindale, Case #09-86-004.

12 Investigation notes, interview with Ken Askew (undated), by Pembina County Deputy Sheriff Joe Martindale, Case #09-86-004.

13 Jean died at age eighty in 1993.

14 *Grand Forks Herald*, March 28, 1986, by Sarah Smith, p. A-1.

15 *Grand Forks Herald*, March 23, 1986, by Sarah Smith, p. A-1.

16 Dean Becker's statement given to Agent Sonny Dump, North Dakota BCI, March 20, 1986.

17 "FBI to join Cavalier probe," *Grand Forks Herald*, March 1, 1986, (*Herald* staff), page not available.

18 "Wahl probe not completed, prosecutor says," *Grand Forks Herald*, August 30, 1986, by Sarah Smith, page not available.

19 *Grand Forks Herald*, August 22,1986, by Sarah Smith, page not available; and August 30, 1986, by Sarah Smith, page not available; and December 13, 1986, by Sarah Smith, p. B-1.

20 "Grand Jury is denied in murder case," *Cavalier Chronicle*, letter from Bob Lee, October 14, 1986, page not available.

21 "National Best Practices," Cold Case Unit,

National Institute of Justice, https://nij.
ojp.gov/library/publications/nation-
al-best-practices-implementing-and-sus-
taining-cold-case-investigation.

22 "Wahl went extra mile for patients," *Grand
Forks Herald*, March 23, 1986, by Sarah Smith,
p. 10-A.

23 "Wahl investigation slows," *Grand Forks
Herald*, March 23, 1986, by Sarah Smith, p. 1.

24 The Mailbag (letters to the editor), *Grand Forks
Herald*, February 22, 1986, page not available.

25 "Cavalier investigators submit Wahl findings," *Grand Forks Herald*, October 9, 1986, by
Sarah Smith, page not available.

26 "Victims of Crime," National Institute of
Justice, https://nij.ojp.gov/topics/victims-of-
crime, retrieved January 15, 2021.

27 Boss, Pauline. *Loss, Trauma, and Resilience :
Therapeutic Work With Ambiguous Loss*. NY:
Norton (2006).

28 James O'Rourke, February 17, 1986 (personal
correspondence).

29 "Murders Increased During the Pandemic,
and the Percentage Solved by the N.Y.P.D.
Plunged," *New York Times*, November
26, 2021 (updated Novemer 29, 2021),
by James Barron, https://www.nytimes.
com/2021/11/26/nyregion/murder-nypd-cas-
es-solved-nyc.html.

30 H.R. 3359 (IH) - Homicide Victims' Families'
Rights Act of 2021, https://www.govinfo.gov/
app/details/BILLS-117hr3359ih.

31 Congress.gov; retrieved November 28, 2021.
    Homicide Victims' Families' Rights Act will
    renew our commitment to support crime
    victims (msn.com) by Billy West, Nelson Bunn;
    Reps McCaul and Swalwell reintroduce bill
    to help families pursue justice on behalf of
    homicide victims (5/19/2021); press release.

32 "GedMatch Implements Required Opt-In for
    Law Enforcement Matching," https://dna-ex-
    plained.com/?s=GedMatch+Implements+Re-
    quired+Opt-In+for+Law+Enforcement+-
    Matching&submit=Search.

33 "We're Entering a New Phase in Law
    Enforcement's Use of Consumer Genetic
    Data," Decemer 19, 2019, by Nila Bala,
    https://slate.com/technology/2019/12/ged-
    match-verogen-genetic-genealogy-law-en-
    forcement.html.

34 "1,300 active cold cases: Here's a look at
    7 active cold cases in Colorado," October
    29, 2021, by Tamara Witty, https://www.
    outtherecolorado.com/features/1-300-ac-
    tive-cold-cases-heres-a-look-at-7-active-
    cold-cases-in-colorado/article_0648162c-
    35e2-11ec-bc38-3b651aca6e28.html.

35 "Could Partial Match DNA Help Solve Cold
    Cases?" May 17, 2021, by Patrick Johnson,
    https://www.msn.com/en-us/news/crime/
    could-partial-match-dna-help-solve-
    cold-cases-bill-filed-on-behalf-of-mol-
    ly-bish-family-would-give-investigators-
    new-tool-but-privacy-concerns-abound/

ar-BB1gOHJY.

36 Combined DNA Index System (CODIS),
    CODIS and NDIS Fact Sheet, FBI.
    gov, https://www.fbi.gov/services/lab-
    oratory/biometric-analysis/codis/
    codis-and-ndis-fact-sheet.

37 *Toronto Sun*, October 15, 2020, by Brad
    Hunter.

38 "Wahl probe will stay open but inactive,"
    Grand Forks Herald, December 13, 1986, by
    Sarah Smith, p. B-1.

39 "Murder vs Manslaughter: What's The
    Difference?" August 6, 2019, by Gabriel
    Quinnan, https://quinnanlaw.com/
    criminal-defense/murder-vs-manslaughter/.

40 *Grand Forks Herald*; December 13, 1986; p.
    B-1; Sarah Smith.

41 *Grand Forks Herald*, March 28, 1986, by Sarah
    Smith, p. A-1.

42 NDCC §44-04-18 (last updated in 2016).

43 NDCC §29-04-01 (2020).

44 OR-Guide.pdf (nd.gov).

45 "Most violent and property crimes in the
    US go unsolved," March 1, 2017, by John
    Gramlich, https://www.pewresearch.org/
    fact-tank/2017/03/01/most-violent-and-
    property-crimes-in-the-u-s-go-unsolved/.

46 FBI data; https://www.pewresearch.org/fact-
    tank/2017/03/01/most-violent-and-property-
    crimes-in-the-u-s-go-unsolved/; March 1,
    2017; John Gramlich.

47 "Public support for the death penalty ticks

up," June 11, 2018, by J. Baxter Oliphant, https://www.pewresearch.org/fact-tank/2018/06/11/us-support-for-death-penalty-ticks-up-2018/.

48 "Less Support for Death Penalty, Especially Among Democrats," PEW Research Center, https://www.pewresearch.org/politics/2015/04/16/less-support-for-death-penalty-especially-among-democrats/.

49 "Unsolved homicides in Lycoming County," March 6, 2021, by Morgan Snook, https://www.northcentralpa.com/news/crime/unsolved-homicides-in-lycoming-county/article_92695766-6f17-11eb-990a-9fe52b-95c3ac.html.

50 Wrigley was asked to resign when Joe Biden, a Democrat, was elected. He resigned February 28, 2021.

51 The *Forum*, June 10, 2021, p. 1.

52 The *Forum*, December 10, 2020, by April Baumgarten.

53 "Feds rejected Alfonso Rodriguez Jr. plea deal to avoid death penalty in Dru Sjodin slaying," Twin Cities Pioneer Press, April 12, 2018, by the Associated Press, https://www.twincities.com/2018/04/12/feds-rejected-alfonso-rodriguez-jr-plea-deal-to-avoid-death-penalty-in-dru-sjodin-slaying/.

54 "Victims of Crime," National Institute of Justice, https://nij.ojp.gov/topics/victims-of-crime.

55 *Grand Forks Herald*, June 10, 1988, by Greg

Booth, p. D-1.

56 "James O'Rourke Blends His Art with His
    Life," *Grand Forks Herald*, November 13, 1987,
    by Greg Booth, p. D-1.

57 "5 Disturbing Unsolved Mysteries In North
    Dakota That Will Leave You Baffled," March 6,
    2016, by Leah, https://www.onlyinyourstate.
    com/north-dakota/unsolved-mysteries-nd/.

58 "Ten years later Russell Turcotte case remains
    unsolved," *Forum* News Service, Grand Forks,
    North Dakota.

CPSIA information can be obtained
at www.ICGtesting.com
Printed in the USA
JSHW021655110822
29137JS00001B/34

9 798985 610512